CAREERS
FOR
CULTURE
LOVERS
& Other
Artsy Types

VGM Careers for You Series

CAREERS

F O R

CULTURE
LOVERS

& Other
Artsy Types

Marjorie Eberts
Margaret Gisler

 VGM Career Horizons
a division of *NTC Publishing Group*
Lincolnwood, Illinois USA

Library of Congress Cataloging-in-Publication Data

Eberts, Marjorie.
    Careers for culture lovers & other artsy types / Marjorie Eberts,
Margaret Gisler.

        p.   cm. — (VGM careers for you series)
    ISBN 0-8442-8134-4 (hardcover)   ISBN 0-8442-8135-2
(softcover)
    1. Arts—Vocational guidance—United States.   I. Gisler,
Margaret.   II. Title.   III. Title: Careers for culture lovers and
other artsy types.   IV. Series.
NX503.E24   1992
700'.23'73—dc20   91-45156
                                                                            CIP

Published by VGM Career Horizons, a division of NTC Publishing Group.
© 1992 by NTC Publishing Group, 4255 West Touhy Avenue,
Lincolnwood (Chicago), Illinois 60646-1975 U.S.A.

Dedication

To Marvin Eberts; Tricia, Mark, and David Gisler; and to James Travers—the music lovers in our families—who have filled our homes with the glorious sounds of music.

Contents

About the Authors

Marjorie Eberts and Margaret Gisler have been writing professionally for thirteen years. They are prolific freelance authors with more than sixty books in print. Their writing is usually in the field of education. The two authors have written textbooks, beginning readers, and study skills books for school children. They have also written a book on preparing children for kindergarten and a college preparation handbook. This is their fourth book on careers.

Beside writing books, the two authors have a syndicated education column, "Dear Teacher," which appears in newspapers throughout the country. Eberts and Gisler also give advice on educational issues in speeches, at workshops, and on television.

Writing this book was a special pleasure for the authors as it gave them the opportunity to meet so many culture lovers who are bringing beauty into the lives of everyone who goes to symphonies, operas, ballets, museums, theatrical productions, and art galleries.

Eberts is a graduate of Stanford University, and Gisler is a graduate of Ball State and Butler Universities. Both received their specialist degrees in education from Butler University. The two authors are also former teachers with more than twenty years of teaching experience between them.

Acknowledgments

We would especially like to thank the following culture lovers who introduced us to the culture lovers whom we wrote about in this book.

Jim Czarnecki
Ken Eberts
Henry Eckert
Ilene Fox
Shelley Henrichsen
Sue Johnson
Sondra Kirshenbaum
Amy Macartney
Pennie Needham
Ron Schwarz
Dr. Jean Sinor
Beulah Steen
Anna Thompson
Patty White
Susan Zurbuchem

Foreword

Art has the power to educate, entertain, and inspire us. Cultural events are a welcome respite from our daily routine, a chance to appreciate the creativity of others, to contemplate new ideas, to reevaluate our own perspective on life. The fine arts offer more than recreation. They enhance the quality of our lives and contribute to our overall well-being.

For culture lovers, there's no greater pleasure than listening to a favorite symphony, going to the opera or ballet, or spending an afternoon admiring the work of a new painter. If you value the fine arts, you may also dream of finding a way to turn your avocation into a career.

Careers for Culture Lovers explores dozens of jobs behind-the-scenes in the fine arts. Music teachers, museum curators, choreographers, and set designers explain how they got started and describe the joys and frustrations of their jobs. They discuss the day-to-day work that keeps symphonies, theater companies, and art galleries in existence and allows the public to share the vision of talented composers, playwrights, and visual artists.

Culture lovers have a unique opportunity to provide that link between artist and audience. Through their work, teachers and arts administrators inspire future artists and create future audiences. Whatever their job description, culture lovers use their skills in countless ways to cultivate in others the same appreciation for the arts that enriches their own lives.

The Editors of VGM

CHAPTER ONE

Jobs for Culture Lovers

*I*s your idea of a perfect Sunday afternoon a leisurely stroll through an art museum, time spent listening to recordings of your favorite symphonies, or several hours viewing a ballet or theater production? Would you prefer viewing an exhibition of Picasso's paintings to watching the Rams or Raiders play a football game? Would it be a highlight of your life to attend a Pavarotti concert or hear Van Cliburn playing Tchaikovsky with the New York Philharmonic Orchestra? Do you dream of watching the Bolshoi Ballet doing arabesques or pirouettes across a stage? Are you interested in studying architectural marvels like the Eiffel Tower in Paris, Saint Peter's in Rome, or the ancient pyramids of Egypt? If you answered a resounding "yes" to any of these questions, you are definitely a "lover of culture."

People who love the arts and culture place them among the things of highest value in their lives. They receive the deepest satisfaction from viewing a masterpiece of art, hearing a fine piece of music, attending an outstanding play, or watching a first-rate ballet. Whether you are a lover of art, music, dance, or the theater; the magnetic pull of culture dominates your life. You may invest your money in prints of the great masters or current pop artists. Perhaps you rush to the music store with your paycheck to buy the latest tapes or CDs. You may even save for months to buy tickets for a ballet like *Swan Lake* or a play like *Death of a Salesman*.

Culture lovers' homes reflect their overwhelming interest in the arts. If your particular interest is music, you may strive to have the finest stereo equipment, and every available space in your living room is probably filled with CDs or tapes of your favorite artists or orchestras. As an art fancier, you may cover the walls of your home with inexpensive prints of famous artists or original oils by fledgling local painters. Or perhaps your walls are graced with pictures of composers, artists, dancers, or theatrical personalities. Culture lovers typically save souvenir tickets and programs of past events in overflowing shoe boxes in their closets.

As children, culture lovers are often involved in classes that teach a specific art form. These are the children who clean their paintbrushes and sharpen their charcoal pencils after spending Saturday mornings learning how to draw or paint at the local art college or museum and then have their masterpieces displayed on the family refrigerator. They are the ones who practice ballet positions on barres attached to the basement or garage wall or fill the air in the neighborhood with oompahs from their tubas and rolls from their drums. They also can be heard singing musical scales or reciting the lines from a future stage production.

Most adult culture lovers are not content to stand on the sidelines when it comes to enjoying the arts. They find time to be artists, musicians, singers, and dancers. For some arts lovers, this means a part time job while for others it is their favorite avocation or recreation. Artists spend hours of their free time painting, sculpting, and making mosaics. Musicians may play in bands, orchestras, and chamber groups in their community. Singers may join choirs or perform with the local opera company. And both singers and dancers often enjoy starring in musical productions.

Career opportunities as artists, musicians, singers, dancers, and actors are extremely limited. Successful careers in these areas require both talent and dedication. Few individuals can reach the stratospheric heights of international acclaim in the arts that Andrew Wyeth, Pablo Casals, Beverly Sills, Jessica Tandy, Laurence Olivier, and Rudolf Nureyev attained. Furthermore, competition is so keen in the arts that only a few people are even able to earn their living entirely from their artistic endeavors. Fortunately, an amazing variety of jobs exists for culture lovers who wish to spend their working hours in jobs closely aligned to their own personal interests. This book is dedicated to helping all culture lovers find jobs that will let them work in areas that they value so highly.

Jobs for Art Lovers

You do not have to paint like Rembrandt, Andy Warhol, or Mary Cassatt to find a job associated with art. Whether you are a curator or a guard, a job in an art museum will bring you into direct contact with fine paintings and sculpture. And you can be a part of the exciting world of buying and selling works of art when your job is at an art gallery or an auction house. As a restorer or framer, you can actually handle paintings. Perhaps your appreciation of art will lead to a job as an art critic. Or maybe you would prefer to work as a teacher helping young people acquire skills in drawing, painting, or sculpting. Upon investigation you will find a wide variety of jobs that will allow you to play an active role in the art world.

Jobs for Music Lovers

Teaching definitely offers the greatest number of jobs in music. The range of jobs is enormous, too—from helping beginners learn to play musical instruments or to sing, to helping experts further hone their impressive skills. You do not have to be a performer to work for symphony orchestras, opera companies, choirs, and theatrical production companies. The larger a musical group is, the greater the number of people required to handle administrative functions and backstage activities. You can have music plus glamour by working for famous soloists and well-known music groups as well as for radio and television stations. With a job in a recording company, music lovers can be a part of creating a tape, CD, or video. Music critics employed by newspapers and magazines combine their love of music with a career in journalism. As a music therapist, you can use music to help people in hospitals and nursing homes improve their health. And of course, there are jobs selling, repairing, creating, and buying musical instruments.

Jobs for Dance Lovers

Dancers express emotion through rhythmic movements as they interpret such feelings as joy, disappointment, anger, and help-lessness. Employment with a dance company offers many jobs to those who wish to help dancers prepare for and present perfor-mances. Behind every dance performance you will find choreog-raphers, costume designers, wardrobe handlers, and stagehands. You will also find some special jobs with dance companies like movement notators who record as many details as are necessary to restage a dance performance. There are also reconstructors who take these details and train the dance company to perform the dance according to the notations, and autographers who put the notations in a form that can be distributed to all the dancers. A love of dance can also lead to a career as a dance therapist restoring people to health through movement. Teaching is an excellent way to share your love of dance with others. Both children and adults are eager to learn ballet, modern dance, folk dancing, and social dancing.

Jobs for Theater Lovers

Whenever the lights go down and the curtains go up, all eyes are drawn to the performers on the stage. Nevertheless, a far greater number of people have jobs behind the scenes of these produc-tions than audiences ever view in the actual performance. For all these productions writers, directors, producers, publicists, business support staff, costume designers, dressers, set designers, hair stylists, prompters, sound and light engineers, and stagehands are required. And when it comes to movies and television productions you need to have all of the above people plus camera operators, film editors, and all the postproduction people. With the advent of the audiovisual industry, cable networks, and computer graphics companies the number of jobs out of the limelight is increasing in the performing arts.

More Jobs for Culture Lovers

Literature, photography, interior design, architecture, and jewelry can also be included within the broad definition of culture. The creators of these aesthetically pleasing art forms require many assistants to produce and sell their finished works. For example, many different jobs like editing, proofreading, typesetting, binding, and layout are involved in producing literary works. Furthermore, in order for the public to have access to the printed word, librarians and booksellers are required.

A vast amount of money is distributed each year by governmental bodies, corporations, individuals, and foundations. Decisions have to be made about which arts groups will receive this money. Culture lovers can find a variety of challenging jobs in the organizations that disburse these funds.

Dream Jobs for Culture Lovers

When culture lovers read want ads, they are always searching for jobs that will allow them to spend more time working in areas that are closely tied to their interests. The following ads would surely capture the attention of many arts lovers.

Dance Therapist   Full time position with prestigious long term care facility. Competitive pay and benefits.

Senior Associate Director   Local university seeks individual to assist the Director of Development in the design, implementation, and management of a program of activities to generate philanthropic gift support to the Museum of Art. Specific responsibility for segments of major gift prospect research, cultivation, solicitation and stewardship activities required for the anticipated capital campaign. Bachelor's degree required, as is at least 4 years experience.

Layout & Paste-Up Person   A publisher of rare and first edition books is seeking an individual familiar with MacIntosh system & 2 color layout/design technique. This person must be experienced & able to work with editors in creating sophisticated artwork.

Public Relations/Communications Director   The American Society of Organists has an immediate opening for a Director of Communications at its national headquarters. The Director is a department head position responsible for production of the Society newsletter and other publications; coordination of media affairs, production and dissemination of press releases and other public relations material. Preferred candidates will have at least 2 years experience in media relations work; experience in desktop publishing; experience with nonprofit organizations and a college degree or substantial coursework in music.

Job Qualifications

Culture lovers appreciate objects and experiences that arouse their senses. A love of culture, while essential, is not sufficient qualification for obtaining many jobs in the arts. Specialized training or academic degrees are required for many of these jobs.   ·
For example, culture lovers wanting to help people through music or dance therapy must combine college courses in music with extensive work in the behavioral and biological sciences. Quite often in the arts arena, a master's degree is a prerequisite

for even being considered for a position. And there are many jobs where holding a double master's degree or a doctorate is necessary to obtain a specific job. Fortunately, a considerable part of the coursework allows most culture lovers to gain more and more knowledge of their favorite art form. And culture lovers seeking careers associated with the arts realize that they must have the best training and education in order to meet the challenges that lie ahead in their careers.

Where the Jobs Are

For many culture lovers, relocation is the name of the game when they are looking for employment in the arts, since the largest number and variety of jobs are found in the major metropolitan areas. In addition, there are certain cities in the United States which are the centers for specific arts such as Nashville for country music, Hollywood for movies, and New York for dance and stage productions. Nevertheless, it is not essential for culture lovers to seek employment in just a few large cities. Scattered across the country in communities of every size there are jobs for arts lovers. For example, jobs in education will be found in even the smallest towns where culture lovers can teach in schools or give lessons in their homes.

For Further Reading

A deeper appreciation of the arts emerges as people learn more about them. There are many excellent guides which will help you become better acquainted with the different arts.

Art

Cole, Bruce and Adelheid Gealt. *Art of the Western World.* New York: Summit Books, 1989.
De la Croix, Horst and Richard G. Tansey. *Gardner's Art through the Ages.* San Diego, California: Harcourt Brace Jovanovich, 1986.

Fleming, William. *Arts and Ideas.* New York: Holt, Rinehart & Winston, 1986.

Gambrich, E.H. *The History of Art.* Englewood Cliffs, New Jersey: Prentice-Hall, Inc., 1988.

Music

Dahlhaus, Carl. *Modern Music.* Berkeley, California: University of California Press, 1988.

Grammond, Peter. *The Harmony Illustrated Encyclopedia of Classical Music.* New York: Harmony Books, 1988.

Hass, Karl. *Inside Music.* Garden City, New York: Doubleday & Co. Inc., 1984.

Mann, William. *James Galway's Music in Time.* New York: Harry N. Abrams, Inc. Publishers, 1983.

Dance

Adshead, Janet and June Layson, editors. *Dance History.* London: Dance Books LTD, 1986.

Balanchine, George and Francis Mason. *101 Stories of the Great Ballets.* New York: Anchor Books, 1989.

Bazarova, Nadezhela and Varvara Mey. *Alphabet of Classical Dance.* London: Dance Books LTD, 1987.

Brown, Jean Morrison, editor. *The Vision of Modern Dance.* Princeton, New Jersey: Princeton Book Company, Publishers, 1979.

Theater

Allison, Alexander W. and Arthur C. Carr, Arthur M. Eastman. *Masterpieces of the Drama.* New York: Macmillan Publishing Company, 1991.

Gassner, John, editor. *Best American Plays.* New York: Crown, 1987.

Hartnoll, Phyllis. *The Theater—A Concise History.* London: Thames & Hudson, Inc., 1989.

Jacobs, Lee A., editor. *The Longman Anthology of American Drama.* New York: Longman, 1982.

CHAPTER TWO

Jobs for Art Lovers

"Art comes to you proposing frankly to give nothing but the highest quality to your moments as they pass."   Walter Pater: The Renaissance

*E*njoying art ranks among many people's most important activities. Art lovers will travel to the Louvre in Paris just to see Leonardo DaVinci's *Mona Lisa*. And when they stand in front of this world-renowned painting, they will not be alone, but part of a group of art lovers sharing this aesthetic experience. It involves their emotions and attention at a deep level, leaving them refreshed and uplifted.

For an art lover, a work of art—whether it is a painting, sculpture, mosaic, mural, or drawing—is not something to glance at for just a moment. Instead, it is something to be studied for pleasure or to learn how the artist felt about subjects such as religion, family, and social justice. Fortunately, for art lovers, the enjoyment of art does not have to be assigned to the role of leisure time activity; there are many jobs which will let them spend their workdays surrounded by art. They can have extremely satisfying careers working in art museums or galleries. Jobs with newspapers and magazines as art commentators or critics give art lovers a chance to share their opinions of works of art with others. Art lovers also have the opportunity to educate both children and adults on artistic techniques and the history of art as teachers.

Art Museums—Paradise for Art Lovers

According to the American Association of Museums (AAM), a museum is an organized and permanent nonprofit institution, essentially educational or aesthetic in purpose, with professional staff, that owns and uses tangible objects, cares for them, and exhibits them to the public on some regular schedule. While this is an all-purpose definition of museum, the word "art" in art museum indicates that these museums care for and exhibit works of art. The focus of art museums varies greatly. An art museum may show works of art from ancient times to the present in many mediums, as the Metropolitan Museum of Art in New York City and the Art Institute of Chicago do. Or an art museum may specialize in the art of one period, artist, or medium. For example, the Museum of Modern Art in New York City is devoted to the collection and exhibition of modern art; the Asian Art Museum of San Francisco concentrates on Asian art from many eras. No matter what specialty interests an art lover, there is probably an art museum devoted to that interest. It is possible for art lovers to find jobs at museums devoted solely to craft and folk art, American Indian, or French Impressionist collections. By reading the *Official Museum Directory* published annually, art lovers can find out just about everything they need to know about individual museums. The directory has information about museum personnel; areas of collections; and the nature, size, and scope of the facilities.

The Louvre, founded in 1793, is generally considered the first real art museum. In the United States, it was not until the end of the 1800s that the number of art museums began to grow rapidly. Today, art lovers will find major art museums in large cities like New York, Boston, Minneapolis, San Francisco, Los Angeles, Chicago, and Philadelphia. They can also find art museums scattered across the country in towns as diverse as Helena, Montana; Akron, Ohio; Utica, New York; Anchorage, Alaska; Andover, Massachusetts; and Sarasota, Florida.

How Museums Work

The purpose of museums is to collect, preserve, research, exhibit, and interpret objects of lasting value for the public, according to the AAM. Museums obtain their collections by buying, trading with other museums, and receiving gifts. The museum staff keeps an accurate record of every object in the museum. The staff repairs and restores damaged objects and employs scientific techniques to protect the collection from deterioration. Most museums store the greater part of their collections for scholarly investigation and only exhibit their choicest objects for their patrons. Museums also offer a wide variety of educational activities including courses, lectures, publications, and guide services.

Career Options in Art Museums

Staff members are needed for a wide variety of positions in art museums—from designing exhibits, soliciting funds, and guarding collections to conducting research, keeping financial records, and sweeping the floors. In large museums, staff members often have duties in a finely defined area, such as curator of Egyptian art. However, in small museums employees need to be "jacks-of-all-trades," capable of handling diverse tasks from training docents to cataloging objects. In all art museums, there is a need for people with sound business backgrounds to run the financial side of the organization. Employees are also needed to handle the clerical and maintenance tasks.

Salaries of individuals working in art museums are similar to those working in other museums. Employees at major museums will usually earn considerably more than those at small museums in towns or rural areas. Salaries will also depend on an individual's level of education and years of experience.

Because art museums are so very different in size, budgets, and collections, the following job descriptions of key personnel give just the basic functions of each position:

DIRECTOR   carries out the policy of the board of the museum and is the manager of all functions of the museum. All staff positions report to the director.

CURATOR   is responsible for the care and interpretation of all objects in the museum and for research on the collections. The curator recommends acquisitions and removals of art works from the collection. Duties may include organizing exhibitions.

CONSERVATOR   scientifically analyzes museum objects to prevent deterioration and repairs them when necessary. The conservator is responsible for keeping objects in the collection at the proper temperature and humidity and protected from pests, pollution, and harmful light exposure.

EXHIBITS DESIGNER   turns the ideas of the museum's curators and educators into drawings or scale models for permanent, temporary, or traveling exhibits. The designer may also be responsible for setting up the exhibit.

REGISTRAR   is in charge of cataloging objects in the collection and maintaining proper documents such as insurance and the copyright and reproduction rights for them. Responsibilities also include the packing, unpacking, shipping, and storing of art objects plus the handling of customs problems.

EDUCATOR   develops, implements, and supervises the formal and informal teaching programs of the museum with the goal of increasing the public's understanding of the art collection. Duties can include in-service instruction for docents, workshops for museum faculty, and the setting up of lecture series, film programs, tours, special events, seminars, and school programs.

DEVELOPMENT OFFICER   is in charge of raising money for the museum through the solicitation of individuals and corporations for donations of money; this person also plans, coordinates, and implements all fundraising programs. Supervising the development staff is an additional responsibility.

MEMBERSHIP OFFICER   has the responsibility of attracting new members, retaining existing membership in the museum, and organizing special events and programs for the members. Duties can include the maintenance of membership records.

The American Association of Museums has also identified the following positions as museum-related jobs:

accountant	gardener/landscaper
archivist	graphic artist
artist	guard
attorney	historian
audio visual technician	instructor
building superintendent	librarian
business manager	maintenance worker
clerk	model maker
computer specialist	personnel director
controller	public relations specialist
curatorial assistant	publications director
editor	research assistant
electrician	sales shop manager
filmmaker	secretary
food service manager	volunteer manager

Job Qualifications

For museum jobs, especially those actively involved in working in some way with the art collection, the key word in getting a job is *experience*. The two best ways to get needed experience are by participating in an internship program and serving as a

volunteer. For art lovers aspiring to positions as directors, curators, educators, registrars, conservators, and librarians a
master's degree in museum studies, the museum's specialization,
or in the applicant's work area is generally expected. For some
prestigious museums only applicants with doctoral degrees are
considered. Bachelor's degrees in business or arts administration are normally required for those seeking employment on
the business side of art museums in such jobs as business manager, development officer, personnel director, and public relations specialist. Being affiliated with museum or professional
associations is a plus for those seeking jobs in art museums.
And since almost all jobs in museums require interaction with
the public, from the guard talking to museum patrons to the
director speaking to the board of the museum, good communication skills are necessary.

Director of a Smaller Art Museum

No one determines what the character of an art museum will
be more than does the director. In Saint Paul, Minnesota, Jim
Czarniecki is the director of the Minnesota Museum of Art; he
has determined that this museum will be people oriented.
Under his leadership, the Museum School offers a formal instructional program in studio art and art history. And the
scheduling of these classes is done to accommodate the variety
of student needs and lifestyles: after work classes for the downtown work crowd; traditional evening hours; and weekend
workshops. The focus of the art in this museum is American
art. Although the museum is people oriented, important research is not neglected. The staff is working on redefining
American art, and through its research is bringing out what
has been ignored or repressed in the past.

   Like most art museum directors, Jim has the responsibility for
hiring and training support staff. Although the Minnesota Museum of Art can be considered a small or mid-sized museum, it
has a staff of twenty six full time employees, fifteen part time

employees, and a faculty of twenty five part time teachers in the Museum School. One of Jim's duties as director is to interpret the Board's policy for the staff and to design programs that will help the staff carry out this policy. Vision is required in the director's job: Jim is involved in setting goals and objectives for the museum to reach in the next three to five years. He is also the chief representative for the museum in the Twin Cities community which requires frequent dialog with community leaders in business and government.

Every day is different for the director of a museum. At the present time, Jim spends 60 to 70 percent of his time working on all facets of the museum's campaign to raise 20 million dollars to build a facility slated to open in October, 1994. Much of his fundraising time is spent talking to members of the Board of Trustees, donors, and key volunteers. One very appealing aspect of working in a museum this size is that Jim is able to stay close to art. He can still curate a show and is able to be intimately involved in building the art collection.

Although Jim was always interested in art and even took oil painting lessons in elementary school, he certainly did not expect to have a career in the arts during high school. His interest then was aeronautics, and he only took one art course in high school. After graduation, Jim spent one year in Antwerp, Belgium, with the American Field Service program. During this year, his interest in art, especially photography, was reawakened. In college, Jim's major was physics, but he spent more time in the photography lab than the physics lab, as he was a photographer for both the newspaper and the yearbook. After graduation, jobs in physics were hard to find, and Jim finally determined that his interest was really photography and art. He elected to look for a job as a photographer.

Between interviews for photography jobs, Jim walked into the personnel office of the Art Institute of Chicago without an appointment, and by the end of the day had a job with the Department of Education writing gallery guides and organizing a film and lecture series for a photography exhibition. Besides working at the Art Institute, Jim also enrolled part time in classes to continue his education in art, especially in photography and filmmaking. Within two years, he was promoted to the position of supervisor of all public programs in the education department. His mentor at the museum allowed him to expand his knowledge of photography even further by letting him take time away from his job to do two internships in photography.

After three years of supervising programs at the Art Institute, the Ringling Museum of Art in Sarasota, Florida offered Jim the job of Director of Education. He took the job because he saw it as an excellent opportunity to try out his ideas of making art more accessible to the public. He succeeded in bringing art to the people by establishing affiliate organizations with other museums in other cities and forming chapters of citizen volunteer groups which sponsored one or two exhibitions each year.

Jim's success with the Ringling program brought him an offer from patrons of the Mississippi Art Association to establish an art museum in Jackson and to serve as its director. They wanted someone who would create a museum that was very responsive to the public. Operating from an antebellum house with galleries in two parlors, Jim was able to help design the new museum and get it operating in eighteen months. Seven years later, the Minnesota Museum of Art asked Jim to serve as director—the position he holds today.

Curators—Guardians of Art

Beyond researching and interpreting the art in their care and arranging exhibitions, curators are the keepers of the art heritage which resides in museums. The number of curators in an art museum is closely tied to the size of the museum. In a large museum like the de Young Museum in San Francisco, the curatorial career path is:

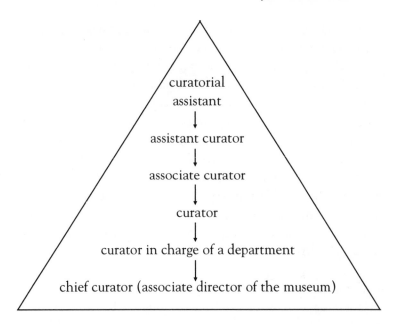

curatorial
assistant
↓
assistant curator
↓
associate curator
↓
curator
↓
curator in charge of a department
↓
chief curator (associate director of the museum)

A similar career path will be found in mid-sized museums; however, in very small museums there may not be any specifically named curatorial positions as the director may also serve as the curator.

CURATOR OF THE TEXTILES DEPARTMENT   Cathryn Cootner is the curator of the textiles department of the de Young Museum in San Francisco. In this position, she has the opportunity to be in daily contact with works of art, looking at them again and again and considering the statements their creators were trying to make even through it is never possible to know totally an artist's message. This aspect of a curator's job should be very rewarding for art lovers.

Cathryn also has the opportunity to look at works of art for possible acquisition by the museum. Like most curators, she has the challenge of coming up with ideas for exhibitions both in the museum and for traveling purposes. Another responsibility is handling her department's internship program by talking to candidates, securing funds for interns, and developing appropriate programs for them. One day a week in her busy schedule is devoted to research. When it is time to set up a new exhibition—which may take up to two weeks—she is there for the installation of the pieces. She generally does not handle the pieces, although curators may do so at smaller museums. She does make sure of where each piece goes and even supervises whether it should be hung higher or lower. Because textiles cannot be hung permanently without being damaged, Cathryn must supervise the rotation of the textiles in the permanent collection at least twice a year, which slightly changes the exhibit's theme. Of course being a curator also involves routine administrative tasks such as handling correspondence, taking phone calls, and arranging schedules.

Curators often have advanced degrees with a concentration in their area of interest. Because universities do not have courses in textile history, curators in this area must build their knowledge through research and working with textiles. Cathryn's interest in textiles emerged during a summer spent in India where she became fascinated with oriental carpets. Subsequently, she started to collect carpets and developed the expertise to appraise and give lectures on them. Her career as a curator began when she was asked by the de Young museum to curate and write a catalog on a collection of nomad and village rugs which the museum had acquired. She began as a part time curator, became a full time curator and then curator of her department. According to Cathryn, there are many routes to a position as curator.

Conservators—Advocates for All Works of Art

Conservators are the experts who are interested only in the welfare of works of art. Their job is to prevent further deterioration and repair paintings, sculptures, books, textiles, rugs, tapestries, picture frames, porcelains, other fine works of art, and cultural properties. Conservators usually have a specialty, since the problems to be resolved in caring for works of art are so difficult that no individual can be an expert in restoring all kinds of art. Preserving a 2000-year-old carving found in the ocean, and preserving a fifteenth century porcelain vase are two very different tasks.

Becoming a conservator is a lengthy process, whether art lovers do it through a formal school program or through an apprenticeship which will last a minimum of five years and usually extends to eight years. There are no undergraduate programs which give bachelor's degrees in conservation. However, it is possible to take technical studies at the undergraduate level and then enter an apprentice or master's program. The first step in the academic approach is to get a bachelor's degree, usually in art history, which should be coupled with undergraduate courses in chemistry, physics, geology, biology, and studio art. Obtaining a master's degree in a conservator's program in some areas of study is quite difficult because of the limited number of schools and limited number of applicants accepted into programs. For example, there are just three schools in the United States that offer a master's degree in fine arts conservation, and each accepts only a very small number of students. Therefore, most students have to wait two to three years to enter a master's program in this area. During that time, they are expected to gain experience working for a conservator. After graduation, they will need to serve an internship. Check your library for a listing of schools offering conservation programs, and you can write to the American Institute for Conservation requesting career information.

American Institute for Conservation
 1400 16th Street NW, Suite 340
 Washington, D.C. 20036

Larger museums have laboratories where conservators work. Smaller museums either tap into the resources of the larger museums or use private conservators. Scott M. Haskins is a conservator who directs a fine art conservation laboratory. His area of expertise in conservation is fine paintings and works of art on paper. Scott's clients include museums of all types, historical societies, corporations with large art holdings, and holders of private collections. Scott trained in Italy and obtained the equivalent of a master's degree in fine arts conservation in Europe which was followed by a one year internship.

In his conservation work, Scott is involved in such tasks as taking water stains out of a seventeenth century drawing, cleaning and repairing rips in paintings, taking acid stains out of water colors, preparing frames for metal leaf, and stopping the deterioration of paintings and works of art on paper. He is interested in every aspect of an art work's welfare. He sees that it is shipped and stored correctly and advises clients on how to prevent light and pollution damage to paintings. Art scholars also use him as a consultant in determining the authenticity of works of art. He was able to tell one scholar that a work of art supposedly by a pupil of Rembrandt's could not be genuine because the whites used in the painting were not invented until 1927.

Scott also has administrative responsibilities. He supervises a conservator and an apprentice with a master's degree in art history and sets up the daily work schedule for the laboratory. A very important part of his job is making sure that all work done on art in the laboratory is carefully documented. In addition, he will spend time talking to clients and prospective clients.

Scott has truly found a perfect career for art lovers as he is preserving what they cherish. The outlook for jobs is good for conservators. Museums seek these highly trained professionals for staff positions or as consultants. Because so much still has to be learned about how to conserve works of art, employment opportunities are also good for conservation scientists who research the effects of such things as pollution, humidity, and lighting on works of art.

Exhibits Designers—Experts in Displaying Art

Exhibit designers do more than prepare works of art for display in a museum; they also prepare the space to hold the works of art. The designers are responsible for the lighting, color of the walls, support graphics for the works of art, audiovisual materials, and flow of traffic, and security for an exhibit. They must also see that the exhibit tells a story with a beginning, middle, and end.

Sherman O'Hara is the chief exhibits designer at the Indianapolis Museum of Art, in charge of installing over thirty exhibits in the museum each year. His work year is rather like show business, "another opening, another show." Each installation begins with a curator telling him or one of the designers on his staff what the story line of the exhibit will be. In many museums, the curator, exhibits designer, and educator will plan the exhibit story together. The next step is for the exhibits designer to plan the actual exhibit, which must be approved by the curator; then a drawing of the exhibit is made. The final step is the installation of the exhibit. This is done by a team including the designer, a lighting technician, someone who mounts the paintings, and other necessary technicians. At times, the museum exhibits "packaged" shows that already come with a story line. In this case, the designer will tailor the exhibit to fit the space.

Sherman has a staff of seven in his department. Three of these people are exhibits designers. When the schedule of exhibits is published for the year, the designers will choose or be assigned to the exhibits which they will do during the year. In the past ten years, the career of exhibits designer has become more professional. There is now a standing committee of exhibits designers on the board of the American Association of Museums. And designers now have a professional organization—the National Association of Museum Exhibitors. There is no specific coursework that is recognized as preparation for this career. Most designers have a bachelor's or master's degree in fine arts with an architectural or design background. As this profession has become more disciplined, there are now opportunities for internships in this area in museums. Sherman now has one intern each year. Being an intern is an excellent way to get experience in this area.

Being the chief exhibits designer means that Sherman has considerable paperwork. He manages his department's budget, handles correspondence, and orders materials. He also has to plan and attend meetings and make sure that exhibits are installed on schedule.

Sherman originally considered a career in accounting and actually graduated as a business major. After graduation, he changed his mind and went to a school of design for postgraduate work. Then he and a partner started a space design business. After they sold the business, he traveled and then took a job at the Indianapolis Museum of Art as chief exhibits designer—the same job he holds today.

Educator—A Performance Arts Coordinator

Anna Thompson learned about a position at the Indianapolis Museum of Art through a newspaper advertisement. The ad read:

"The Indianapolis Museum of Art has an opening for a full time music performance arts coordinator. We are seeking an experienced educator with a background in music and/or music and film to research, develop, and implement the music, film, and performance arts programs for the museum. Many programs are designed in conjunction with educational programming for the permanent collection and special exhibitions. Concerts and film series are presented on weekends and evenings. Masters in music or related fields are highly desirable. Three to five years university or high school teaching experience or equivalent. Background in film study or art history also desirable. Strong oral, written, communication, and organizational skills required. Send cover letter and resume to . . ."

Anna had been a school music teacher for three years, had an advanced degree in library science, plus experience in organizing educational programs at the library and making arrangements for a meeting of the National Conference of Music Librarians which qualified her for the position. She applied and was hired. Her job involved dealing with several media—art, music, and film. Anna researched and developed programs related to specific art exhibits. She selected films for the summer film series. In addition, she put together family programs and programs that were sent out to the schools. When the museum's new pavilion opened, Anna commissioned a work by a composer to reflect the artist's work in the exhibition. In this job, she also did grant proposal writing to obtain funds for the performing arts programs. In carrying out her job, she worked closely with the museum's curators.

Deputy Director for Development

The Fine Arts Museums of San Francisco include the de Young Museum for American art and the California Palace of the Legion of Honor with a European collection. Housed in two buildings, it is one of the largest museums in the United States with a budget of 13.5 million dollars a year. The development office has a director, an associate director, and two deputy directors who are in charge of all unearned revenues—grants and contributions from individuals, corporations, foundations, and government agencies. The directors have the responsibility of running a program that instills good relations between the museum's benefactors and the museum.

Jim Forbes is a deputy director at the Fine Arts Museums of San Francisco. While he was working on his doctorate in music history, Jim decided he did not want to stay in the academic world as a teacher but preferred to work in arts administration. For him, the idea of working in a development office was especially appealing, as he realized the importance of funding to the continued operation of programs in all the arts. He became more aware of the important work done by development officers by volunteering in the development office of the university while he was a graduate student.

Jim first secured a job as chief development officer with a small ballet company. A friend in the development office of the university told him about this job opening. Jim made his next career move to the development office of the Nelson Atkins Museum in Kansas City because he was interested in working in the visual arts. A search team called him about the job opening for his current position as deputy director of the Fine Arts Museums of San Francisco.

The directors of the development office do not do any direct fundraising at the Fine Arts Museums of San Francisco. Instead, Jim works with board members and board committees who actually do the fundraising. Jim and his staff of four do all the support work for the fundraisers. They educate the board about the museum's needs, prepare brochures to tell the museum's story, create mail solicitations, plan special exhibitions, and devise the year's fundraising strategy. And when corporations give gifts, Jim's staff finalizes the agreements. Art lovers who want to find a career that really supports the operation of museums will find careers in development offices to be very rewarding.

Human Resources Manager at the Walker Art Center

Almost every member of the administrative staff at the Walker Art Center in Minneapolis, Minnesota, is an artist who brings an artist's sensitivity to his or her position. Wendy Lane, the human resources manager at the museum, is no exception. Art is so important to her that she lives in a studio with both living and work space. She meets once a month with other artists so they can critique each other's work.

In her job as human resources manager, her primary responsibility is recruitment. When a new staff member is needed, she writes the job description and then sees that the opening is publicized. This involves sending the posting to about 350 arts and service organizations as well as placing ads. Wendy handles the response by reviewing resumes and working with the supervisor of the open position to decide who will be interviewed. The supervisor does the initial interview, and Wendy does the final interview before they get together to make a decision. The demand for positions at the very prestigious Walker Art Center is huge. Hundreds will apply for every position, especially since many artists want to work at art museums. Just having a background in art is not a sufficient qualification for most positions. Applicants generally need to have a bachelor's degree, with advanced degrees preferable for many positions.

Beside her recruitment responsibilities, Wendy is in charge of new employee orientation. She talks to new employees about the museum's policies and procedures and signs them up for benefits. And when an employee leaves, she will do the exit interview and the paperwork on the termination. As part of her job, she has written the policy and procedures booklet and created an employee appraisal form which is tied to annual salary increases. She also makes up salary guidelines which are approved by supervisors. Wendy wrote the museum's affirmative action plan and makes sure that it is being followed. It is also her job to respond to discrimination issues. Wendy's responsibilities include serving as liaison between employees and management and managing the personnel procurement budget and the personal services budget for things that benefit employees in general.

The opportunity to obtain a job as human resources manager in an art museum is limited because only museums with 100 or more employees will need a full time staff member in this position. Quite often, this position is coupled with that of administrative director. While a salary of $25,000 to $30,000 would be paid for human resources managers at art museums, the same position in for-profit organizations would command a salary of between $40,000 and $60,000.

With a bachelor's degree in arts administration, Wendy had the academic background necessary for obtaining an administrative job at a museum. But she also had an additional strength—

business experience from being the co-owner of a health food distribution company. Wendy answered a newspaper ad for a secretary at the Walker. Her prospective boss also wanted someone who could handle the human resources part of his job and thought she would be able to do this. Within one year, she was an administrative assistant, and three years later she was the human resources manager. Wendy's career path shows how a fulfilling career in an art museum can develop from an entry level position.

Art Galleries—Working Amidst Art

Art lovers can purchase sculpture, etchings, antique prints, original fine art, tribal art, serigraphs, and limited edition graphics at art galleries. They can also find jobs working in art galleries, for there are thousands of them in the United States. Furthermore, there is such a diversity in galleries that art lovers can look for a job in a gallery that sells art according to their favorite medium, style, period, or artists.

Art galleries can be as dissimilar as, on the one hand, a small showroom in a tourist resort selling paintings and sculpture by local artists versus a 10,000 square foot loft in a high rent district in New York city selling paintings worth millions of dollars, on the other. Wherever art lovers choose to work, it is essential that they have a knowledge of art. At many galleries, this means having at least a bachelor's degree in art history, and for some galleries having a master's degree is required even for entry level positions. In New York City, competition is so intense that job seekers try to get a foot in the door by working as interns for no wages or minimum wage, or by taking the most lowly job available at a gallery.

Director of a Small Gallery in a Suburban Village

What started out as a part time job in a small gallery has turned into a full time job as director of the gallery for Dianne Wright.

When Dianne first started to work at the gallery, half of the inventory was antique furniture and the remainder was nineteenth and twentieth century paintings, with a few eighteenth century pieces. As the owners of the gallery acquired exceptional estates which had paintings by renowned artists of the region, the gallery emerged as solely an art gallery which promoted the paintings of regional artists, past and present.

According to Dianne, working at a small gallery is like being part of a family; it is not just a business. As director, she has many duties which office managers have, but she also is constantly doing work associated with the art. Dianne handles her own clients and makes public presentations to educate clients and corporations about regional artists. This requires research work on her part—an agreeable task for art lovers. She also consults with private and corporate clients who want to start an art collection, which means talking to them about their interests and visiting their homes and offices to see the environment for the paintings. Dianne also keeps a "want" list for clients and notifies them when she finds a painting. Some of her time is spent corresponding with clients, other galleries, and museums.

Dianne does not have a bachelor's degree in any area of art. She had originally planned to become a commercial artist but became disenchanted with this field and switched her major. Her qualifications for her original job at the gallery were experience in an office job, an interest in art, and skill with people. It was on-the-job experience that earned her the job as gallery director.

Owner of a Gallery in New York City

Major art galleries in New York City are extremely selective in choosing entry level employees. Armed with a bachelor's degree in art history plus experience as a summer intern at the Metropolitan Museum of Art, Tim Nye went around to art galleries with his impressive resume looking for his first job. He found a job as a gallery assistant at Nancy Hoffman Gallery, where he handled art, made boxes for shipping, sent out packages, labeled slides, and went to clients' homes to hang art which they had purchased. There was no glamour in this job, but it was a beginning for Tim. His next job was as a cataloger at Robert Miller Gallery. A cataloging job involves taking photographs of art and writing the serial numbers on the back of the work. This was a particularly appropriate job since Tim had written his thesis on one of the artists whose work was sold at this gallery.

Tim went away from the art world briefly to get an MBA with a concentration in nonprofit organizations. He knew that he always wanted to return to the art world and did so during the summer after his first year of graduate school. With profits made from selling two paintings by a pop artist whose work swiftly escalated in price after the death of Andy Warhol, Tim was able to mount his own exhibition. He rented a temporary gallery space and put together a showing called "Three Painters." One of the painters was a friend, Paul Pagk, who had received recognition in France. After graduation from business school, Tim found a fabulous 7500 square foot open loft. He was also able to obtain funding from a foundation for two one-man shows in his loft gallery. Each show was hung for about six weeks, longer than the typical one month show in New York City. The success of previous shows allowed him to find funding for a third show, the works of a sculptor. Tim is trying to make his gallery a center for contemporary arts and is holding poetry reading and concerts in the gallery. As far as the future goes, Tim hopes that he will be selling art and continuing with his gallery.

An Artist's Representative

Both commercial and fine artists often need someone to bring them jobs. This is the role artists' representatives play: they sell artists' talents to people in a position to pay for the use of their talents. Shirley Talbert works full time as a representative for commercial artists. Although she works in a firm that has another representative, most representatives work alone. To find companies that need commercial artists, she calls on art directors in advertising agencies, graphic designers, and corporations, talking to them about their needs. Her clientele is decidedly not a fixed group, with new people always needing her service; neither is the group of artists she represents. Commercial artists call Shirley or send her resumes of their work. She evaluates their artwork and tries to sign contracts for at least a year with the artists she decides to represent.

Much time and effort is required to market the work of an artist. Shirley works with the artist to create a portfolio that displays his or her distinctive style which she can then show potential users of the artist's work. When a client requests an artist who can do a certain type of work, Shirley usually visits the client with the portfolios of three artists who have different styles. Her job as an artist representative does not end when an artist is selected by a client. She is responsible for seeing that the artist's work is completed on time and to the specifications of her client.

Shirley also works part time on her own as a fine artist representative. In this role, she finds a client first and then looks for an artist after spending considerable time consulting with the client on his or her needs. Being an artist representative requires both business and art backgrounds which Shirley has. Her business experience is derived from working in marketing after she graduated from college with a bachelor's degree in sales and marketing. Shirley acquired her knowledge of art through collecting paintings and graphics.

Art Appraisers Value Art Works

People often want to know the value of a work of art for buying or selling the piece, or sometimes just to satisfy their curiosity. In addition, they may want information for insurance, tax, or family division purposes. The experts who decide the price or value of artwork are called appraisers. This career requires really knowing art and the value of individual pieces of art.

Karen Tallackson was about eighteen when she decided that she wanted to be an art appraiser. To acquire the necessary background in art, she obtained both bachelor's and master's degrees in art history. She also studied art in England and France where she had direct contact with many works of fine art. To begin to have an idea of the value of different pieces, she read such periodicals as *Connoisseur, Art News, Art in America,* and *Fine Arts and Antiques.* To gain more knowledge of art and valuing art, she started at Butterfield & Butterfield, a firm of international fine art auctioneers and appraisers, as an intern. Today, she is an appraiser with this company. Her internship project was to create a chronological dictionary of California paintings. This helped Karen become familiar with the artists and their styles, as well as previous auction prices of their works. When her internship was completed, Karen became administrative assistant to the director. This allowed her to become familiar with the clientele of the auction house and auction procedures. After she expressed an interest in contemporary art, the firm let her start making appraisals from photographs of contemporary art which were sent to the firm for evaluation. In her next position as inventory manager, she inventoried every piece of art that came into the firm by entering it into the computer. This meant she was actually seeing and handling works of art. According to Karen, the more art a prospective appraiser sees, the more skilled the individual becomes in making qualitative judgments. She also learned more about the market by talking to clients. One way prospective appraisers can find out more about the job is by contacting the American Society of Appraisers which has an organization that students can join. This organization also gives accreditation to professional appraisers. For more information about appraising contact:

American Society of Appraisers
  P.O. Box 17264
  Washington, DC 20041

After the contemporary art appraiser left the firm, Karen became Butterfield & Butterfield's contemporary art appraiser. One of her duties is to make insurance appraisals. She also finds properties for the firm's semiannual contemporary art auctions. She acquires properties for these sales from all over the country, which means spending considerable time on the phone. When a piece arrives at the firm, Karen sees that it is photographed and enters information about it on the computer. For each auction, she will create the catalog which will describe the artist, the work of art, and the pre-auction estimate. Appraisers must know the market so Karen is always going to galleries and openings plus reading *Journal of Art* and *International Art Newsletter* to keep abreast of pricing and market trends.

Being an appraiser is an opportunity for art lovers to have daily contact with art. Besides requiring an excellent knowledge of the media which the appraiser values, phone and computer skills are essential, as is an ability to deal with people.

An Auctioneer of Fine Art

An auction at Butterfield & Butterfield is a sale at which people bid for fine art, antiques, jewelry, and collectibles. One of the auctioneers is Bernard Osher, who is also owner and chairman of this firm. To prepare for an auction, he must be aware of what is being sold. This means studying the catalog for the auction and learning which items are most important. It also involves talking with department people about the items to be auctioned.

You do not go to school to become an auctioneer. Instead, you learn by watching other auctioneers and then developing your own style. A very important characteristic for auctioneers is confidence in themselves. Before Bernard Osher became an auctioneer, he was an art collector. He had attended many auctions and became an auctioneer as soon as he and his partner purchased the firm.

Art Critics Bring News on Art

According to David Bonetti, art critic for the *San Francisco Examiner*, art critics can be divided into two groups. In one group, you will find the critics who write for art journals. Their audience is assumed to be knowledgeable about art, so jargon can be used in these critics' pieces. The other group of art critics write for daily or weekly newspapers with large circulations. They cannot assume that their readers have any more than a basic knowledge of art, so they write in a straightforward way, reporting on what is happening in art. Some newspaper art critics just report the facts. Others, like David, write more about what artists are trying to do and whether they are successful in achieving their own goals. He also feels it is important to explain to his readers what the newest art is all about.

Unlike music and theater critics on newspaper staffs, art critics seldom have a deadline. It is not as important for them to report immediately on the opening of a new show at a gallery or museum because people will have many opportunities to see the show. Not having the pressure of a deadline gives the art critic time to reflect on a new show.

As sole art critic for the *Examiner,* David writes three or four columns a week for the paper. His job should be very appealing to art lovers because he spends considerable time looking at art in museums, galleries, and other places which exhibit. Much reading about art is required in his work. For example, a recent exhibit of Indonesian art at a museum had a 400–page catalog which David had to study to learn about the background, history, aesthetics, and cultural context of the exhibit. In the case of contemporary art there is rarely a catalog, so he must research his response to the art—which may itself become part of a future catalog.

Unfortunately, there are not a great number of jobs for art critics at newspapers, since only major newspapers will have full time critics. In addition, the outlook for more newspaper jobs for art critics is not rosy. The number of newspapers in the United States is steadily dropping. There are approximately 1000 fewer newspapers today than in the early 1900s. Furthermore, many major newspapers are losing circulation to suburban papers.

There is no one career route to becoming an art critic at a newspaper. It is not something that can be studied at school. Obviously, an ability to write and a knowledge of art are basic requirements. Many art critics, according to David, started out wanting to be artists or writers—especially poets—and then redirected their interests to critical writing. However, David's route to becoming an art critic did not develop in this way. After majoring in literature and taking many art courses in college, he taught preschool—specializing in art and literature. From teaching he went to work in sales at an art gallery. While working in the gallery, he started writing art reviews for a monthly publication. He heard of an opening at a Boston paper for an art critic, sent them his clippings, and got the job. His next career move was to his current position in San Francisco. "Being an art critic," David says, "is being paid to work with my interest." It is decidedly not a nine-to-five job for him. Even on off days he is at galleries and museums pursuing his interest in art.

Art Teachers Inspire Art Lovers

While a very limited number of art students ultimately become professional artists, most gain an appreciation of art through their classes in school. Art lovers who wish to share their love of art with others will find teaching art to be a rewarding career.

Teaching lets practicing art lovers introduce future art lovers to different media and the history of art and artists through the ages. Individuals wishing to teach art in public schools will need bachelor's degrees in education with training in art education. Most will also obtain their master's degrees early in their teaching careers. At the college or university level, having a doctorate is a prerequisite for all art teachers except those who have attained acclaim as outstanding artists.

Art lovers wishing to teach in elementary school will find that the current demand for art teachers is reduced in many areas because of budget cutting. At the high school level, fewer art teachers are needed in many states because more required courses have been added to the curriculum, which means fewer students can choose art classes as electives. Competition for positions teaching art in colleges and universities is as intense as it is in all other areas of instruction at this level.

ART FROM THE CART   Sonia Fernandez is an elementary school art teacher. She has taught in beautiful, fully equipped art rooms, in cafeterias, and science rooms; she has also pushed a cart loaded with art supplies from room to room. Teaching art can be a hectic experience in an elementary school. Art teachers never seem to have enough time to get everything done. Supplies have to be taken out and put back for each class, and a project must be completed in thirty or forty-five minutes. According to Sonia, an hour would be an ideal amount of time for an art class, especially for students in the intermediate grades, but this rarely happens. Art lovers planning to teach art should also realize that they may see every student in the school during the course of the week. This often means teaching art to more than 500 students. Art teachers also have demands made on their time to prepare such things as posters for paper drives and props or scenery for a school musical or play, plus helping children participate in art competitions. Add in the frustration of crowded classrooms, and you might wonder why Sonia enjoys teaching art and would not think of teaching any other class. The reason is simple: She thoroughly enjoys introducing young children to the world of art.

A LIFETIME OF TEACHING ART   Jim Doversberger always knew he wanted to be an art teacher, and that is the one and only job he has ever had except for a short stint in the navy. Jim brings a solid knowledge of art to his teaching career, since he has both bachelor's and master's degrees in fine arts. He took education courses and did student teaching to qualify for his teaching credential. While attending Herron Art School, he taught art classes every Saturday morning. He continued teaching these classes for many years after he became a full time teacher because he liked teaching classes to children of different ages.

Jim first learned of his future teaching job from a notice on the bulletin board at the art school. Prospective art teachers can still learn about positions in this way, as well as through college placement offices and even newspaper ads. Jim applied for the job and was hired as an art teacher. When he first started at Lawrence Central High School, he was the only art teacher at this small suburban high school. Over the course of his career, the suburb grew and the art faculty expanded until there were six art teachers, and Jim was department chairman. The number of art teachers was reduced when another high school was built in the district and further reduced to one full time position and one part time position when fewer students began to take art because of increased requirements in science and social studies.

A typical course load for Jim would be teaching beginning art, drawing, and graphics; intermediate drawing and painting; and advanced art. His classes would average twenty six students at the beginning level, but as few as twelve on the advanced level. On the intermediate level, Jim would always devote Friday to teaching art history. He and the other art teachers in the district had the opportunity to develop their own curriculum within the broad guidelines of the state requirements. Most experienced teachers will be able to develop their own curriculums in this way.

Art teachers, like other teachers, have responsibilities that extend beyond the classroom. Jim sponsored an art club at times throughout his career; in the early part of his career, before a stagecraft teacher was hired, he designed the stage sets for the school's two annual productions. When an empty room turned up at the school, he established an art gallery which featured constant shows of the students' art work. Much time every year was devoted to helping students prepare for major art competitions. He was also on the board of the regional scholastic art competition. Some of his time was also spent judging other art competitions.

Jim spent considerable time painting at the start of his teaching career. Then this lover of the arts switched his interest to the local theater and appeared in over sixty five plays. Teaching does give art lovers time to pursue their interests in the summer. Jim has been to Europe eight of the past ten summers visiting art museums. He also has attended workshops during the summer.

Additional Career Options for Art Lovers

Wherever a collection of art is located, there exist possible jobs for art lovers. Art lovers should investigate the possibilities of working at corporations because these places, like museums and art galleries, may have art collections which require curators, conservators, art historians, and librarians. For example, the First Banks System in Minnesota, Bank of America, and Goldman Sachs & Company all have sizeable art collections which are predominantly displayed in the firms' hallways and offices. Curators of collections in the corporate world, besides loaning pieces to employees for their offices, often launch programs to educate employees about art.

Today's libraries also offer job opportunities for art lovers. Many libraries have programs which involve the loaning of works of art. In addition, librarians with a knowledge of art are needed in the art departments of major libraries.

Beyond the world of fine art, there is the rather large world of commercial art. You can imagine the size of this world when you think of all the commercials that bombard you from billboards, newspapers, magazines, catalogs, and radio and television stations. In each of these arenas, there are scores of employees dealing with the development of commercial art designed to sell products to the public. Many jobs, especially in advertising agencies and commercial art studios, involve working directly with art.

Whenever art lovers see art that appeals to them, they are also seeing job opportunities in buying, selling, displaying, and choosing this art. Being involved in art is not just a job for its creators.

CHAPTER THREE

Jobs for Music Lovers

M usic is one of the oldest arts forms. People were probably singing as soon as they developed language, and by approximately 10,000 B.C., they were making primitive musical instruments out of hollow bones. Today, music plays an important part in many social and cultural activities as well as occupying a major role in opera, ballet, motion pictures, radio, and television.

While music is a performing art, few individuals are able to support themselves as full time performers. Many music lovers elect to combine performing with jobs that allow them to be closely associated with music in the workplace. They can be employed as music teachers, music therapists, copyists, recording engineers, instrument restorers, disc jockeys, librarians, booking agents, publicists, salespersons in music stores, employees at record and video companies, and an amazing variety of other jobs closely associated with music. Just a glance at the music section in the Yellow Pages of your local telephone directory will give you an idea of the number of companies in your community that are connected with music.

Teaching Music

Teaching music is an excellent way to share a love of music with others—from fledgling musicians in preschool to skilled graduate students in a university. Since each age level offers different challenges and rewards, prospective music teachers will need to decide which age group is most appealing to them. At all levels, music teachers in schools have a number of duties that must be performed from taking attendance to giving grades. In addition, there are frequently state, local, or school guidelines which prescribe the curriculum that is to be taught in music classes. Besides normal teaching duties, most music teachers will usually spend time before and after school working with different musical groups or preparing students for special contests and performances.

You can learn more about careers in teaching music by contacting the following organization and requesting information on careers in music.

Music Educators National Conference (MENC)
1902 Association Drive
Reston, Virginia 22091

You can also learn more about the profession by studying professional journals like these publications found in university libraries and some public libraries:

The American Music Teacher

The American String Teacher

Music Educators' Journal

The Choral Journal

Contributions to Music Education

Beside information on teaching, a few of these journals have some job listings for music teachers. Libraries also have state publications concerned with music education which will frequently have advertisements for teaching positions.

Elementary and secondary school music teachers normally hold a bachelor's degree with a major in music education. During the course of their teaching careers, many will also obtain master's degrees. Current funding difficulties in the public schools, coupled with the fact that music is not considered a basic subject, have led to a tighter job market for prospective music teachers. Individuals seeking employment as music teachers usually learn of job opportunities through college placement bureaus, employment fairs, newspaper advertisements, and networking with other teachers. Many also contact school districts to see if there are positions available for music teachers.

College and university music teachers who teach theory classes are usually required to have a doctorate in some aspect of music; however, exceptions are made for those who teach performance classes if they have the press clippings to demonstrate a national reputation in their teaching area. Competition is extremely intense for positions at this level, and many qualified people are competing for few jobs.

Teaching in an Elementary School

Julia Scherer has taught music at the same elementary school for over fifteen years. She plans to stay at this school until she takes early retirement to publish the school musicals she has written and to make commercials. Not able to find a job as a music teacher after graduation from college with a bachelor's degree in music education, Julia applied for a job as a substitute teacher— only to find the district was looking for a music teacher. She applied for the job, was hired, and is still working at this school. Like most music teachers, Julia has obtained a master's degree in music and taken other additional courses.

As an elementary music specialist, Julia teaches general music classes which feature instruction in vocal music, composers, music reading, instruments of the orchestra, music appreciation, and playing the recorder—depending on the grade level of her students. Outside of her hours at school, she spends time planning and presenting three major musicals, two spring sings, and choir and recorder ensemble programs each year. Twice a week, she comes in early to give special instruction to the ensemble groups. Most elementary school music teachers will have similar responsibilities.

Inspired by her elementary and high school music teachers to choose a career as a music teacher, Julia transmits her love of music to her students. She was introduced by one of her former students who had a major role in the musical *Cats*, to the cast backstage, as the lady who got him started in music. Knowing her students appreciate her efforts is what makes her career so satisfying.

Julia resembles most music teachers in that her involvement with music does not end in the classroom. Over the years, she has directed children's church choirs, given private voice lessons, sung with an entertainment company, and starred in numerous community theater productions, receiving many awards for her singing and acting ability in these shows.

Teaching in a Junior High School

It is a challenging job to create an orchestra, choir, or band from a group of students in sixth, seventh, and eighth grades. Many of these students have never sung a note or held a musical instrument in their hands before their first day in the music classroom. This is a challenge that faces junior high school music teachers like Joe Zaharako every day.

Joe is the band director at a large junior high school. His teaching responsibilities include teaching band to students in sixth, seventh, eighth, and ninth grades, along with a general music class for sixth graders. Other teachers at this school concentrate on teaching choir or orchestra along with a few classes in general music. At smaller schools, music teachers should expect to teach both vocal and instrumental music classes.

One of the most appealing aspects of Joe's job is seeing how his students develop as musicians during the four years they spend at the school where he teaches. Most school districts will not have the sixth grade as part of the junior high school, and increasingly there are middle schools with just seventh and eighth grades.

Joe's educational background includes a bachelor's degree and a master's degree in music education, the typical education pattern for music teachers. His time spent with music is not limited to teaching; he is also a member of a brass choir.

Teaching in a High School

Thomas Dick was not born into a musically inclined family; his father did not even recognize a cello when his son brought one home. However, from an early age music just seemed like the natural thing for Thomas to do. He became a very skilled cellist, playing first chair in several community orchestras. During college, he made the decision to become a teacher rather than a performer because he wanted to help young people. He was able to pay for his education with a music scholarship plus jobs as a cellist with a symphony orchestra and as a string bass player in a group that performed at supper clubs. Thomas also played in the orchestra for roadshows like *Fiddler on the Roof* and *Sound of Music*. You will find that a great number of music teachers earned part of their college costs through working as performers.

Since completing his bachelor's degree in music education, Thomas has taught at three high schools, obtaining his master's degree in music education along the way. In his present job, he is the Director of Orchestras at a large suburban high school. He teaches four periods of strings and one period of wind and percussion each day. During a typical strings class, he will begin by having the students play scales for intonation, quality of sound, and technique. Most of the period will be devoted to working on problems with current pieces, with some time devoted to sight reading and the teaching of musical terms, abbreviations, and signs.

The day is long for a high school music teacher. Four days a week, Thomas supervises rehearsals of different sections of the orchestra after school; every Tuesday evening he holds a three hour rehearsal of performance and possible contest pieces to discover problems that the students can work on at home and in their sections. Thomas receives a stipend for the work he does with students beyond the regular school day, as most high school music teachers do.

During the school year, he will be the guest conductor for junior and senior high school orchestras and act as a judge at several music contests. He also finds time to serve on the board of the state school music association. In the summer, Thomas will often act as the orchestra director of a summer music camp. Today, when this busy music teacher has time, he sings in a church choir. During his teaching career, he has also at various times played the cello with different symphony groups and directed choirs.

Thomas's goal is to give his students a good experience in his orchestra classes, which he hopes will lead to a lifetime of enjoying good music and the playing of a musical instrument. He sees himself as being a student-oriented music teacher rather than a performance-oriented teacher. Because he is so sensitive to the needs of his students, the walls of his office abound with plaques and letters of appreciation, like the following one from his orchestra students when he left their school for his present position:

A Tribute to the Conductor

As our teacher, we have both loved and admired him, for he has been much more than a simple instructor. Not only has he been the key to our musical growth, but he has been our friend and our inspiration as well. Through him we have been encouraged to better ourselves both with music and in our daily lives.

As our conductor, he has shared with us his wonderful gift of music. Through his help and guidance we have each been allowed to develop our inner talents into a product that we can use to bring joy to others.

Teaching in a College

Martin Marks dreamed of being a performer as a child—a dream he realized by playing the piano with symphony orchestras and giving solo recitals in the Midwest. Besides performing, he also gave piano lessons to as many as 100 students a week, plus studying for his bachelor's and master's degrees in music with a performance orientation. His outstanding reputation as a teacher and pianist led to his appointment as a part time and then a full time professor of music. Today, his schedule includes giving classes in piano literature and performance anxiety as well as teaching piano to college students and a few private students.

Private Music Instruction

Being a private music teacher is an excellent way to combine teaching and a love of music. Working in their homes, students' homes, and studios, these teachers usually instruct school-aged children. How many students a teacher will have depends on the demand in the area as well as the individual's reputation as a skilled teacher. Since most of their students are in school during the day, a private teacher's work day does not normally begin until the end of the school day. Fees usually range from $10 to $20 per lesson, although some experts command fees as high as $150 per lesson.

PRIVATE TEACHER   With an educational background of a bachelor's degree in music education with a minor in music therapy and a master's in performance, Melissa Williams has taught music in elementary school and worked at a residential treatment center for emotionally disturbed children. Today, she teaches tuba, euphonium, and trombone to about forty students, plays in symphony orchestras in two cities, and does some freelancing at recording studios making music tapes. To get started as a private teacher in a new city, she joined a brass choir and played with a local symphony, where she met many school music teachers who have recommended her to students in their classes. In her free time Melissa practices the tuba, hoping to win an audition to be a regular in a major symphony orchestra. To hone her skills this accomplished musician takes lessons from an expert player with the Chicago Symphony.

Music Therapists—Helping People through Music

Music therapists are a bold, aggressive group who are pounding on doors of hospitals and other treatment centers, explaining how adding a music therapist would enhance the facility. Although people have been helped by music through the ages, it is only since the 1950s that music therapists have been slowly accepted by the medical profession as a part of its treatment team. The National Association for Music Therapy, Inc. (NAMT) describes music therapy as the use of music in the accomplishment of therapeutic aims: the restoration, maintenance, and improvement of mental and physical health.

As a result of their efforts, music therapists are now being added to the staffs at some hospices, nursing homes, rehabilitation centers, prisons, school systems, clinics, and day care and treatment centers for children. At the same time, due to current budget restraints, many music therapists are being forced to take jobs with titles like activity or program director—which means that music is only a small part of their jobs.

Music therapists do not just work in institutions. Freelance music therapists continue working with patients who have been discharged from a hospital, easing their adjustment back into the community. Therapists also work in their studios with young children and adults who have been referred to them by health professionals.

As members of a treatment team, music therapists work with doctors, social workers, occupational therapists, nurses, and psychologists. As individuals, the team members meet with new patients and assess how their discipline can help these people. Then the team meets and discusses the role each discipline will play in helping in the patient's recovery and sets goals for the treatment plan. The committee will meet again every few months to review each patient's progress. The music therapist will use music and music activities usually in a group setting to bring about desirable changes in behavior. Since music has a great effect on people's feelings and emotions, it helps the patients share their thoughts with others in a nonthreatening way.

Qualifications

Music therapists need to be emotionally stable individuals who can work well with both their clients and the personnel of the therapeutic treatment team. They will also find it helpful to be able to play more than one musical instrument. To become a music therapist a bachelor's degree in music therapy with courses in music, music therapy, psychology, and the social sciences, followed by a six month internship at an approved treatment facility, is required. After completing the degree program or equivalent and internship, a music therapist can apply to become a Registered Music Therapist with the National Association for Music Therapy. Registration shows that he or she has met the organization's rigorous educational and clinical training standards. To become board certified, music therapists must take a national music therapy examination which is recognized by the National Commission on Certifying Agencies. This insures that board certified music therapists have the highest professional qualifications.

The salary range for jobs as music therapists is from below $20,000 to slightly over $40,000 a year. Benefits will vary greatly depending on the facility where a therapist works. Many jobs in state and federal facilities offer the benefits of civil service positions.

A Music Therapist's Job

After learning more about music therapy, Barbara Romerhaus switched her major from music education to music therapy because she enjoyed helping people and liked working in hospital treatment facilities. She concentrated on piano and flute in college, but then learned to play the autoharp, and different percussion, string, and woodwind instruments in order to be able to help future patients through using a variety of instruments.

Barbara's first job was as acting director of music therapy at a state hospital. She could not be appointed director because the facility required two years of experience for appointment to this position. Barbara worked a forty hour week setting up patient choir groups, teaching musical skills groups, and helping patients tap into community resources when they left the hospital. It is an important part of the job for music therapists to find music groups in a community where discharged patients can go to continue their music interests.

Barbara's next job was on a research project in a psychiatric hospital, doing a study of autistic children under the guidelines of a major university. Like all research studies, the program was very structured and research oriented. Barbara worked with ten autistic children teaching them various motor skills, concepts like "up and down" and "right and left," and even numbers and letters—through music and song. According to Barbara, music helps people learn and remember information better than any other medium because of the structure within it. Music was also used as positive reinforcement toward attaining a desired behavior change. The autistic children responded positively to the music and were rewarded by being able to listen to favorite songs. Some of the children had language skills, while others let Barbara know their musical preferences through body language.

After two years with the research program, Barbara became the director of the hospital's adult music therapy program for the adult psychiatric program. Her duties were now quite similar to those of her first job at a state hospital. She conducted classes in such areas as music and relaxation, music and movement to help increase the patients' energy and motivation, and music and recreation to help patients acquire leisure skills.

After an eleven year break in her career path to raise a family, Barbara returned to music therapy at a state hospital—illustrating that a career in this profession can be resumed after even a break of more than a decade. Today, she is the rehabilitation therapy supervisor at the hospital with twelve people under her supervision, including two music therapists, two occupational therapists, a recreational therapist, and therapy assistants. Her duties include administering, planning, and making sure that the programs her staff are conducting meet the needs of the patients. She also has to make sure her staff works within the allotted budget, and she attends hospital administrators' meetings. In addition, she is in charge of the music therapy internship program at her facility.

Music Librarians

Libraries with large collections of music books, recordings, musical scores, and periodicals associated with music have jobs for music librarians. The focus of music collections in public libraries is usually general, with materials ranging from popular to classical music. Some libraries, like the Library of Congress and the New York Public Library, have so much information about music that they serve as research centers. Academic libraries have more scholarly materials than most public libraries, and some will specialize in a particular area, like the jazz library at Rutgers University. Music librarians can also find jobs at places which have large music collections which need to be kept in order— such as radio and television stations, large music publishers, and professional music associations.

It is not easy to become a music librarian. Most music librarians have master's degrees in library science from an accredited program of the American Library Association. For many positions, they are also required to have master's or even Ph.D degrees in some aspect of music. The salaries that music librarians can expect to receive range from $15,000 to $30,000 according to the Music Educators National Conference.

Music lovers do not have to have advanced degrees to work in music libraries, as there are jobs there for clerks who usually have completed technical or associate degrees in library science. However, almost everyone working in music libraries will work with library clients, so skill in interacting with people is another job requirement.

A Music Librarian

Equipped with a bachelor's degree in music education, Anna Thompson spent three years teaching music before returning to college to earn a master's degree in library science. She obtained her job as a music librarian in a major midwest city through an interview held at her college. Because the music library was large, the music librarians specialized. Anna was in charge of all the sound recordings and cassette tapes, and she made selections of scores to be added to the band and ensemble sections. Part of her duties consisted of developing educational programs for the general public and the schools. For example, she organized a series of woodwind recitals. This task required her to compile a bibliography, select performers, finalize contracts with them, and handle the publicity for the event.

Most professions have associations which allow members to extend their knowledge of the profession and to network with others in the field. Anna found further satisfaction in her career by being very active in the Music Library Association. She chaired the public library committee and served as chair for local arrangements when the association met in her city.

Symphony Orchestras

When the conductors of the more than 1500 symphony orchestras in the United States raise their batons to begin a performance, there are always people behind the scenes seeing to the orchestra's management. The larger a symphony is, the greater the number of people required to handle such administrative tasks as raising funds, marketing, publicizing the group, negotiating contracts, and handling the finances. Although jobs with these orchestras are very appealing to music lovers, the number of jobs is definitely limited: there are only thirty major symphony orchestras. Job titles and responsibilities will vary depending on the orchestra; however, music lovers are likely to find the following or similar administrative positions with major orchestras.

MANAGING DIRECTOR   has responsibility for all aspects of operating an orchestra and must implement policies of the symphony board.

OPERATIONS MANAGER   assists the managing director in the operation of the orchestra.

DIRECTOR OF DEVELOPMENT   is in charge of all fundraising programs.

BUSINESS MANAGER   handles all financial matters.

PUBLICITY DIRECTOR   deals with the press and manages all aspects of promoting an orchestra.

DIRECTOR OF EDUCATION   works with schools in developing concerts and other educational activities.

TICKET SERVICE DIRECTOR   is in charge of the sale of tickets.

Besides these top management positions, music lovers can find at least seventy more jobs at major orchestras as part of the administrative staff. Fewer jobs will be available at medium-sized orchestras, while smaller orchestras may employ only a manager who is assisted by volunteers. Community orchestras may just employ a part time manager or be completely run by volunteers.

Symphony orchestras hiring administrative staff look for individuals who have a background in music coupled with bachelor's or master's degrees in business or arts administration. Music lovers who want to work in this area will find it easier to get jobs if they have worked with a symphony as a volunteer or intern.

Working as Director of Development

Raising money is never an easy job, but that is the number one responsibility of directors of development for symphony orchestras. They plan, coordinate, and implement all fundraising programs. Sponsoring cocktail parties, gala dinners, symphony balls, and other special events are some of the ways that directors of development raise funds. They may also initiate direct mail campaigns and telethons as money raisers. Time must also be spent searching and applying for business and government grants. Since volunteers play such an important role in soliciting funds, development directors must devise programs to recognize their invaluable help. Part of the director's job is to approve all newsletters, news releases, and fundraising literature. And the director must also supervise staff and run the department within the budget.

Herbert L. Jones has been involved in professional fundraising and public relations for more than thirty years. Currently, he is vice president for development with the Indianapolis Symphony Orchestra (ISO), a post he has held since September, 1989.

As head of development for the ISO, one of the nation's few full time, 52–week season orchestras, Herbert Jones is responsible for all fundraising and supporting programs, with priority focused on the capital gift program designed to raise $50 million in new endowment funds within the next few years.

Prior to joining the ISO administration, Herbert Jones served four years at Butler University as vice-president for university relations. His other previous experience includes heading development programs at Iowa Wesleyan College, Albion College, and Garrett-Evangelical Theological Seminary. He has also acted as a consultant in fundraising for a number of organizations and has several publications on fundraising to his credit.

Working as Publicity Director

While the musicians are busy playing and the director of development is trying to raise funds, the publicity director is telling the media about the orchestra and promoting future symphony performances. Newspapers, magazines, radio stations, and television stations have to be notified about special events such as children's concerts and holiday specials. Stories must be followed up so that the director or one of the staff members can see if additional interviews or photos are needed.

At the Indianapolis Symphony Orchestra, the position of publicity director is called Media Relations Manager. For the past two years, this job has been held by Tim Northcutt. He is a music lover—an absolute requirement for this position. Tim can still recall the incredible experience that he had attending his first lollipop concert (a symphony program for children). His love of music continued in college where his roommates were music majors and he became hooked on opera.

Courses in journalism and political science helped Tim obtain his first job in public relations, working as media secretary for a congressional candidate during his senior year in college. Successful work on this campaign led to stints as a reporter covering the Indiana General Assembly and campaign jobs for governors, senators, mayors, and congressmen in Kansas, California, Texas, Minnesota, Arizona, and Florida.

Desiring to stay in one place after marriage, Tim accepted a job at the Tampa Bay Performing Arts Center, a huge $57 million complex, that holds over 800 performances a year within its three theaters. At the Center, Tim dealt with all kinds of entertainers, from comedians to opera stars. The Center wanted Tim for this position because of his media background in dealing with *Time*, *Newsweek*, the Washington press corps, and major television networks during political campaigns. Tim wanted the job be-

JOBS FOR MUSIC LOVERS   53

cause of his love of culture and saw it as an opportunity to create a better understanding of the arts.

In his current position as media relations manager for the Indianapolis Symphony Orchestra, Tim handles media relations with local, regional, national, and international press, along with telling the ISO story to the public. While the administrative side of the symphony operates like a typical corporation, the organization is quite innovative on its artistic and programming side. For example, the orchestra holds the Symphony Promenade, which is like a stroll through a park in Vienna, and Symphony on the Prairie, where people can relax on the ground with a picnic and enjoy the music. There is also the Indiana Bells, a yuletide celebration. ISO was the first orchestra in North America to do a multidiscipline holiday show. Tim handles the publicity for all of these events. He looks forward to coming to work each day because there are always new challenges in his job.

Performance Librarian—A Job with Music

While an administrative job supports the functioning of a symphony orchestra, the job of performance librarian involves working closely with the orchestra and the music. These librarians' comprehensive knowledge of music, combined with their library skills, helps them perform their duty—which is to get music to the musicians. First, they obtain the music from the orchestra's library or buy or rent new music. Rented music must then be returned when the orchestra is no longer using it. Once the music is obtained, the performance librarian is responsible for getting the music ready for the orchestra by adding the bowings and all the different marks that will be necessary. Often the librarian works with the conductor and soloists in the preparation of the music. The librarian must also attend all rehearsals and concerts at home and on tour, to make sure that the music is handed out to each musician and then collected after each performance. This is definitely not a job with regular hours like music librarians in libraries have.

Michael Runyon is the performance librarian for the Indianapolis Symphony Orchestra. He began playing the piano in first grade and later picked up the trumpet, French horn, and harmonica. During his high school years, he became interested in composition and began composing and arranging for the school swing choir and jazz band. He went on to study composition in college and says that most college programs allow the study of both classical composition—for symphonies, ballets, and operas—and commercial composition—for jingles, film scores, and television shows. His love is classical composition. Throughout his college years, Michael worked as a copyist, arranger, and studio musician; he also played in bands, taught at universities, worked in art groups, and wrote grants. Michael holds a bachelor's degree in composition and a master's and a doctorate in composition. Because of his musical background, he can customize parts for the orchestra and analyze scores for them.

Michael, with the help of two full time and one part time performance librarians, gets the parts ready for the individual symphony players. When the orchestra buys or rents music, it is never ready for the musicians' stands as it comes out of the package. Often the music has been written for more or fewer instruments than the Indianapolis Symphony has. Then decisions have to be made whether additional musicians will be brought in, whether some musicians will be allowed to go on holiday, or whether some musicians will be assigned extra parts. The principals of each section and the conductor mark the music to indicate changes so that everyone in each section will be reading the same music. Michael and the other performance librarians see that these changes are made for each musician.

As a performance librarian, Michael needs to be preparing music years in advance of its presentation as well as honing details for compositions soon to be performed. His duties also extend to working on cost analysis of proposed concerts and answering questions such as how many musicians will be needed and whether soloists will be required. Michael likes working with the production of a concert. He is able to handle the pressure of

The Publishing Side of Music

Adding to the diversity of jobs in the music world is the publishing side of music—including the publication of books and magazines on music, instruction books for different instruments, sheet music, and school textbooks. Music lovers who want to work in the book and magazine side of publishing need to couple a knowledge of music with writing skills. There are magazines for almost every musical interest, so music lovers have the opportunity to spend their days writing about their favorite form of music whether it is classical, country, opera, or heavy metal.

Publishing Sheet Music

Every piece of sheet music that musicians use has been published by a music publishing company. There are large publishing houses as well as small, independent music publishers. Many individuals start out with large companies and then leave these companies to start their own firms. Other publishing houses are launched by writers of hit tunes to sell their own music.

No matter what their size, the first job of music publishing companies, large and small, is to select music that will sell. This is an important knack that determines how successful a company will be. One hit popular song can make a very large amount of money for a music publisher. Once a publishing company decides that a piece of music is saleable, contracts are negotiated with the writer and the material is copyrighted. The music is put in the right form for printing and then distributed.

A SHEET MUSIC PUBLISHING COMPANY   Scott Houston and his father have found a unique marketing niche in the music publishing business. They are educational music publishers who sell band and choir arrangements for use in schools, instructional books for music instruments, and manuscript paper. Their three-year-old firm has four employees. Scott has the responsibility of evaluating submissions from personal acquaintances and other people who know what type of music the company publishes. He contacts the writers of saleable music and offers them a standard royalty contract. Next, the company obtains the copyright for the music. Then the music is sent out to a music engraving company which prepares the piece for printing. Scott does the layout and the prepress production work and the music is printed in-house. For sixteen weeks of the year, Scott and his father are on the road separately, going to conventions and visiting stores so retailers will know their product.

Copyists Prepare Sheet Music for Publication

Music copyists transcribe each individual musical part from a score onto paper. For example, a copyist will go through a complete score and write out the entire part for the flute, making it much easier for the flautist to play his part. Traditionally, copying has been done with a special technical pen, with the same process followed for each musical instrument. Just as the computer has changed other areas, it has revolutionized copying music. Copyists can now play on a keyboard directly into a computer. The information is then translated into printed notations. This is a very quick process, and with the aid of a modem, copyists can quickly send completed scores anywhere in the world to music publishers and other groups needing their work. Most copyists will either own their own businesses or work for music publishers.

BLUE NOTE ENGRAVING   In their free time, Jeff Wiedenfeld and his wife Julie run Blue Note Engraving, a company that copies music. Their company is fully computerized, and the speed of the computer is very important in getting music to the clients on time. According to Jeff, the computer does it all. Publishing houses, music groups, and composers need copies quickly and with the modem he can get copy to a publisher—even one in London—without much delay. Julie and Jeff do no copying by hand because they have instructed the computer to do it all. Although their business is based in the Midwest, they have clients throughout the country.

Publishing School Music Textbooks

School children do not just use textbooks for mathematics, history, and reading; they also use textbooks in their music classes. Larry Hillman is the executive editor for music at Silver Burdette and Ginn. In this position, he is responsible for both creating the company's music materials for kindergarten through eighth grade and for supervising a staff of fourteen editors—all of whom are musicians and former music teachers. As part of his job, Larry speaks with both teachers and students to determine what type of product each grade level needs. Dreaming up the product is the creative side of his job. The administrative side includes supervising his department, making business projections, overseeing the budget, and dealing with sales and marketing. An appealing aspect of this job for Larry is being in direct daily contact with music, since he supervises the recording of every song used in the series.

In studying Larry's career path to his present job, music lovers can see other job opportunities which they might like to explore. Larry's first job was as a music teacher. His qualifications for this job included playing the piano and organ since he was in second grade and holding both bachelor's and master's degrees in music. He also had a minor in business, which turned out to be very helpful in his career. After teaching music from kindergarten through junior college for ten years, Larry became a music consultant with Silver Burdette; this was both a sales and service job. He would present the company's products to the teachers and then go back and help the teachers learn to use the materials after a school had purchased them. Larry was next promoted to product manager of music, essentially a marketing job. He had to come up with advertising campaigns and help oversee research and product development. Before becoming executive editor,

Larry was a program editor who had supervising responsibilities and did direct editing of music materials.

The Recording Industry

The recording side of music represents a multibillion dollar industry which produces all the cassettes, CDs, tapes, and records which music lovers buy in order to listen to their beloved music. Today, there are more than 2000 companies producing and selling music—which adds up to a considerable number of jobs for music lovers. There are giant corporations such as CBS, RCA, Warner, MCA, and Polygram which produce almost every type of music and have a large stable of artists. On the other hand, there are very small companies which may only produce one type of music or the music of a few artists. The three leading cities for recording music are New York, Los Angeles, and Nashville, although companies are scattered throughout the United States. The largest companies will have offices in several cities.

The making and selling of a recording, whether it is a cassette, tape, or CD is a complicated process. At the giant corporations, individuals work in a specific area such as promotion, marketing, sales, or publicity; at smaller companies employees tend to have their hands in almost every aspect of producing and selling a recording. What follows is a description of the people who are involved in producing a recording and exactly what their role is so that music lovers can see what jobs might appeal to them in the recording arena.

ARTIST AND REPERTOIRE DEPARTMENT (A&R)   This is the group that finds talent as well as the music which an artist or group will perform. The music may come from a staff writer, the artist or group, a new arrangement of an old favorite, or a demo sent to the company. A&R works with the producer in planning all the details of the recording, from the number of musicians to choosing a recording studio (large recording companies no longer have in-house recording studios but instead use independent studios). A&R is also in charge of the budget for a recording, which includes paying the bills and keeping financial records. In reality, A&R seems to be in on almost every decision about a recording. The department works with advertising, promotion, public relations, and marketing to determine the game plan for releasing a recording.

ART DEPARTMENT The design of album, tape, and cassette covers plays an important role in the selling of recordings. Designers, graphic artists, and photographers work on their creation.

PROMOTION, PUBLICITY, AND ADVERTISING A well integrated plan has to be developed to catch the eyes and ears of the prospective buyers of recordings. The greater the audience who reads, listens to, or hears about a new recording, the greater the chance it will be successful. This means getting radio stations to play the recording, talk show personalities and music critics to interview the artist or group, scheduling television appearances and press conferences, and buying advertisements in all the media. It may even include coming up with a gimmick such as a special t-shirt, pin, or hat.

SALES AND MARKETING Marketing strategies have to be developed to get recordings into the hands of the consumer. This involves close work with promotion, publicity, and advertising as well as setting up displays in stores and visiting or calling stores, music directors at radio and television stations, and music columnists at newspapers and magazines.

Music lovers desiring to work for large recording companies will find having a degree in some field of business or music business helpful in securing a job. Working as an intern or in an entry level position can give job seekers the experience most recording companies expect them to have. Jobs can be learned about through contacts in the field and ads in newspapers and trade papers like *Billboard* and *Cashbox.*

Recording Studios and Recording Engineers

It has been said that there is a recording studio on almost every corner in Nashville. Recent advances in technology have made it possible for small studios to produce excellent sound recordings. Today, music is often recorded at certain studios because of the expertise of the recording engineers who work at, use, or own these studios. No matter how excellent an artist, act, or the personnel at a recording company are, the success of a recording also depends on the end product which the recording engineer creates.

Recording engineers operate the sophisticated equipment used to make recordings. Their job begins with the setting up of the equipment for a recording session to produce the sound that they want. During the actual recording session, they must push the right buttons and switches to get the desired sound. Finally, and this requires considerable skill, they must mix the recorded tracks down to either two or four tracks. At times, a recording is made at several studios—even in different cities. For example, the rhythm bed may be laid down in one studio and the vocals at another while the sound is mixed at yet another studio.

Some recording engineers hold bachelor's degrees in electrical engineering. Others may have completed courses at vocational/technical schools, and some learn by serving as apprentices. There is a great deal of competition for positions as recording engineers. One of the best ways to secure a job is by serving as an intern. Although these engineers may begin by earning no more than minimum wage, successful engineers working for name performers or groups can easily make $100,000 a year.

AIRE BORN   Mike Wilson and John Bolt are partners who own Aire Born, a recording studio located in the Midwest. They rent studio time plus their expertise as recording engineers. The two have created a successful business recording commercials, albums, and corporate materials. Fifty percent of their work comes from servicing a small niche in the recording business—sheet music publishers. These clients want recordings to demonstrate the sound of their sheet music to potential customers.

Mike and John traveled slightly different paths in becoming recording engineers, although both feel they gained their expertise through hands-on work experience. Mike obtained a degree in music business and went to a recording workshop during college. While in high school and later on, he played in a rock band that had its own eight-track recording studio, which gave him practical experience in sound recording.

John, on the other hand, went to a technical school as a part of high school and took a course in sound engineering. After high school, he also attended a recording workshop. The workshop then offered him a job which gave John his work experience in the business. In his next job, he worked at a studio owned by a sacred music writer and demonstrated his expertise by making three gold records in the religious market. Mike and John met while working at different studios and quickly found that they shared similar values as well as the goal of owning a twenty-four track recording studio. They decided to mortgage their homes and start Aire Born which has proved to be a successful venture.

EARMARK MUSIC WORKS   Johann Sebastian Bach wrote music to order for patrons. In the same way, Doug Benge and Pete Schmutte, owners of Earmark Music Works, create music for clients, usually advertisers. The first step involves talking to the client to find out what the music is to accomplish—the desired image or mood. Then Doug or Pete will use a computer program as they compose a piece of music with or without words. The musical notation program transmits what they play on a keyboard to notes which they can see on the computer screen. They remove the floppy disk from the computer, go into their recording studio, put the disk into a computer and assign their newly composed piece to different synthesizers using two software programs to create the music in a rough form. The client listens to the music, and any necessary changes are made before the final product is recorded.

Composing has certainly changed since Bach's time. Like Bach, both of these modern composers are musicians who share a great love of music and have always played in bands. Both have impressive academic credentials. Pete holds a master's degree in music composition, and Doug has a bachelor's in philosophy and a master's in English.

The Retail Side of Music

Music lovers are good customers of retail stores selling records, tapes, CDs, sheet music, and musical instruments. These stores can also be pleasant places for them to work with music frequently drifting through the air plus customers who share the music lover's interest in music leading to many congenial conversations on different aspects of music.

Owners and managers of retail music and record stores must have a solid knowledge of music as well as of business. While a college education is not required, courses at this level can provide a good background in both music and business. Salespersons need to be knowledgeable about music and skilled in dealing with customers. If they work in a store selling instruments, it is a decided plus for them to be able to play one or more instruments. Being a salesperson is a good way to enter the retail side of music. With experience, salespersons can advance to managerial positions or even to owning their own stores.

MANAGER OF A MUSIC STORE   Jeff Wiedenfeld manages Frank's Fiddle Store in Indianapolis which sells, rents, restores, and repairs string instruments. He secured this job through a friend who was a bass player. The owner has been an orchestra teacher in the Indianapolis Public Schools for many years, and his shop is well known in the area. As the manager, Jeff is responsible for the general and administrative parts of the business. One of his duties is to price instruments that the store sells on consignment and those that are being traded in for better instruments. The store also does restorations of string instruments which literally means getting the instruments back in good health. Jeff especially enjoys this aspect of his job and can frequently be found in the workshop cosmetically restoring or as he calls it "coloring" an instrument. Jeff has learned this craft through trial and error. Now he is busy creating a violin which will take over 400 hours to make. His first violin will be a treasured possession that he will never sell; however, if all goes well his second violin might be for sale.

Glamour Jobs in Music

You can combine your love of music with a glamorous career in the limelight or behind the scenes when you have a job in radio, television, and movies, or with rising stars and superstars. Perhaps you could be one of the many people in the background helping famous musicians like pop star Michael Jackson or violinist Isaac Stern perform. On the other hand, you can grab part of the limelight for yourself with a job as a personality playing music from country to classical on radio or commenting on operas and symphonies to radio and television audiences or even introducing music videos to MTV viewers.

Radio and Music

Wake up in the morning to the sound of music drifting from your clock radio. Hop in the car, and drive with music easing the boredom. Jog along a path with music from the radio setting the rhythm of your stride. Wherever people go, their radios go with them; and much of the time, the radios are tuned to music programs. Depending on the organization of a radio station, the individual selecting the music can be the program director, the music director, the on-air personality, or someone holding some combination of these titles. No particular educational requirements exist for these jobs; however, knowledge of music is definitely a prerequisite. Most people currently working at these positions began their careers in small radio stations working at any job they could find or through a college internship. The typical career ladder is from on-air personality position (also called disc jockey) to music director to program director and from small station to larger station at every job change.

MORNING PERSONALITY   Scott Fischer is the morning personality of WENS, working the 6 A.M. to 10 A.M. shift at this all-music radio station in Indianapolis. For twenty-five years, Scott has worked as an on-air personality. Sometimes he cannot believe that he is paid to have such fun in the morning. The pay for being an on-air personality can be quite good; the average income for this position is currently $105,000 a year, with some personalities earning several million a year.

Music has always played an important role in this music lover's life. As a child, Scott collected and listened to records, besides playing the mellophone and French horn. It seemed natural for him to select a career which combined music with his other love—radio. At college, Scott majored in theater and communications, a useful background for individuals seeking employment in radio. However, Scott really got his first exposure to the radio business in college by working at the campus radio station and a local radio station on weekends and during the summer. After graduation, Scott spent several months scouring the smaller radio markets for a job as a disc jockey personality, sending his resume and demo tape to stations. While most on-air personalities begin their careers at small market stations working for salaries close to minimum wage, Scott secured a job in a medium market station in Des Moines. From Des Moines, he went to Denver to work as on-air personality and music director, for more money and at a better time slot—the typical career path for on-air personalities. After Denver, Scott worked in major radio market stations in Chicago and Atlanta before securing his present job in Indianapolis.

On-Air Personality and Music Director   J. D. Cannon of WFMS in Indianapolis, a country radio station, prepared for his career as an on-air personality by attending a vocational/technical school after high school and studying broadcasting for a year. Part of the curriculum at the school was technical training, and part was announcing. J. D. learned of his first job from another student at the school who told him about an ad for an afternoon news anchor at a Madison, Wisconsin, radio station. From this job, J. D. went on to become an on-air personality at the same station.

In his current job, J. D. is also the music director, a position which requires the ability to judge and predict which new songs will become popular with listeners. Each week, J. D. has to sift through approximately fifty new songs to select the four or five which will be added to the rotation at his station. This is a time-consuming job which begins on Monday, when he spends two or three hours on the phone talking to promoters. On Tuesday, he enters all the music into the computer to create the computer generated play list for the week. Songs have to be categorized by J. D. according to their current popularity so that the computer program can create the printed list detailing when songs will be played and how often they will be played. J. D. uses information from research companies, music charts, and publications like *Radio and Records, Billboard,* and the *Gavin Report* to determine such things as which songs are hot locally and which songs are starting to lose popular appeal. On Wednesday, he listens to all the new products and decides which ones to insert in his previously adjusted computer list.

Because J. D. is an on-air personality, he must also spend time each day preparing for his daily program, which includes chitchat about music and information on artists and concerts between thirty minute segments of nonstop music. In addition, he spends time on Thursday and Friday making commercials for the program. Away from the radio station, J. D., like other on-air personalities, spends considerable time doing personal appearance work at parades and shopping malls.

PROGRAM DIRECTOR   Ed Lennon held a wide variety of jobs— from selling cars to owning a fire alarm company—before he began working in radio part time selling ads. Quickly, the radio bug bit, and Ed found he was spending more time at the station fooling with the equipment and writing and producing commercials than selling ads. His next job was as a part time producer of a radio show at another station. He proved himself by working forty and fifty hour weeks at his part time position. Soon he was pushing the buttons and cuing up the records for Dick Clark's syndicated show.

At every opportunity, Ed always volunteered and took on more responsibility, which led to a temporary full time position producing commercials and then to the job of production director responsible for the production of all commercials and promotions at the station. Being willing to work hard throughout his entire career helped Ed obtain his present job as program manager for WIBC—a large station in a major market area where he supervises the on-air staff and shapes and directs the on-air sound, which includes the task of choosing the right music for WIBC's audiences.

A Music Critic

Imagine the satisfaction for a music lover of being involved vicariously with music through writing about concerts, reviewing records and CDs, and interviewing music presenters and musicians. This is the job that Jay Harvey has as a classical and jazz music critic for the *Indianapolis Star,* and it seems like almost a perfect job for music lovers. With a background of trombone playing, a bachelor's degree in English, and a master's in teaching; Jay entered the teaching profession. After a few years, he decided on a different career path and went into newspaper work. For fifteen years, he reviewed classical music, visual arts programs, and some theater productions for the *Flint Journal* in Michigan, as well as writing book reviews and general features for the paper. Wishing to concentrate on music, Jay moved to his current paper where he is a music critic.

A typical work day, which begins at 2 P.M., might involve writing a review of *Porgy and Bess* which he saw the previous evening, completing a piece on the labor and management problems of the local symphony orchestra, listening to recordings which have been sent to him to review, and writing short announcements about music activities throughout the state. During a usual work week, Jay will attend three or four musical performances, illustrating the varying days and hours that music critics work. Job requirements for the position of music critic on a newspaper include having a good ear and an excellent knowledge of music plus good writing skills. Besides finding jobs at newspapers, music critics also work for magazines of the music genre.

Managing Musical Stars and Groups

A personal manager is a deal maker who oversees all aspects of an individual's or a group's musical career. This involves dealing with record companies, music publishers, booking agents, and merchandisers. It also means handling the promotion, publicity, touring, and concert logistics for the artist or group. Then there is the all-important job of managing the act's money. Finally, the personal manager must work constantly to develop the act's career and an audience for the act's music. For handling this wide variety of jobs, a manager makes from 10 to 50 percent of an act's gross; the typical manager takes from 15 to 20 percent. Working with a top artist or group can mean an income of over $500,000 a year. Most personal managers usually handle one artist or group. There are also companies which handle several artists or groups and divide the responsibilities among a staff of professionals.

The one qualification successful personal managers have in common is an excellent knowledge of how the music industry works. Contacts within the industry are also extremely important in launching and maintaining and act's career. Furthermore, personal managers need to have a very good personal relationship with the individual artist or act. At one time almost all personal managers were located in New York or Los Angeles. While this is where most managers still are, many personal managers now live in the same area as their artist or group.

Managing a Rising Star   If you are familiar with the rock hit, "Hey Baby," then you know that Henry Lee Summer is the artist responsible for this song. The personal manager helping Henry Lee Summer go all they way to the top is James Bogard, who brings his considerable knowledge of the music industry to this task. During high school, James had his first introduction to the industry when he played in a professional band. After graduation from the Berklee College of Music in Boston, he learned even more about the music world as a performer with a soul group crisscrossing the country for over five years. During this time, he acted as the eleven-member group's liaison with their manager, who taught him what was involved in being a manager through almost daily phone calls. He also had the opportunity to learn how to deal with nightclub owners, public relations people, and booking agents. After the group broke up, James became the manager of the rhythm section of the band and got the new band up and working, to the point of being offered a recording contract, but he could not keep the group together.

James then worked at a recording studio where he met artists who wanted to make their own records, including Henry Lee Summer. Henry Lee impressed James because he had talent, drive, and determination to go to the top. James left the studio and concentrated on Henry Lee—helping him with his records, booking his nightclub act, and working with him on recording projects. Then he became Henry Lee's personal manager and began to handle all aspects of this rising artist's career, including arranging for his client to be interviewed on popular television shows like "David Letterman" and "Arsenio Hall" and overseeing the companies which Henry Lee owns. Top artists like Henry Lee usually have their own publishing, touring, and production companies and may have a record and even a movie company. Daily, James deals with all the people who want to interface with Henry Lee on different projects. James also has an assistant who handles Henry Lee's personal financial planning and investments. Although James no longer performs, he enjoys working in the music industry overseeing Henry Lee Summer's career. He is also developing a couple of acts which are not yet commercial.

Booking Entertainers for Special Events

Joe Deal is owner of Joe Deal Events, a company that does special event planning. His company handles every aspect of an event and can even come up with the theme or promotional idea for the function. Joe has a roster of talent that includes bands, musicians, and entertainers of all types. He matches what his clients are looking for with the talents from the roster.

Joe obtained a bachelor of science degree in a music business program. This is a relatively new degree program, which Joe liked because he could combine his love of music with business courses. To get this degree he needed not only four years of study at college but also had to complete two internships. He did one at a booking agency and the other at a music store.

Music and Jobs with Churches

In churches and temples, music is an important part of religious worship from the rhythm of African drums to the melodic voices of the Mormon Tabernacle choir. For music lovers who have a knowledge of church music and a desire to work in a religious setting, there are jobs for music directors and choir directors.

Qualifications for these jobs usually include a bachelor's or master's degree in church music plus an ability to direct music performers. Full time jobs in these positions are often limited to churches and temples having large congregations. About the only other jobs in this area are as assistants to music and choir directors.

DIRECTOR OF MUSIC   Robert M. McBain, D.M.A. is presently director of music at Carmel Methodist Church. He has an impressive academic background with bachelor's and master's degrees in music as well as a doctoral degree. In addition, he has an instrumental conducting degree from the Mozarteum in Salzburg, Austria and has done postdoctoral study with Donald Neuen at the Eastman School of Music in Rochester, New York.

As the son of a Baptist minister and an accomplished vocalist, Robert's first association with music was closely linked to his involvement in church music programs. Today, he has strong personal feelings about sharing his musical talent with his church. Throughout his years of study, Robert stayed involved with church music and also worked in the school system teaching choral music in secondary schools. Today, even though he is director of music, supervising all the music programs in a large church, he is also a general vocal music teacher in the public schools. Robert points out that the salary for his job varies greatly depending on the church. For example, in some large churches in major cities music directors can earn as much as $100,000 annually. However, he wants music lovers thinking of becoming church music directors to realize that it may be necessary to supplement their income, as he has done through the years with his teaching.

As director of music at his church, which has 2,600 members, Robert manages a staff that includes a part time children's choir director, a full time organist, and a music associate. Besides the paid staff members, there are also a number of volunteers. Robert has been the music director of several other churches and has had staffs of 50 people reporting to him as well as being the only musician on staff. In many churches, the music director is also the choir director and organist.

In addition to his responsibilities as church music director and teacher, Robert is also director and conductor of the 150-member Carmel Symphonic Chorale and executive director of Music at Carmel, Inc., which puts on monthly concerts for the community. In the past, this versatile musician has been guest conductor at symphony orchestras in Oklahoma, Phoenix, Atlanta, and Indianapolis. He has also been the bass soloist for the Robert Schuller Hour of Power, sung with the Robert Shaw Choral, and recorded several albums.

CHOIR DIRECTOR   Choir directors have the responsibility of directing the choir for church services. Directors also hold auditions for positions in the choir and work with section leaders, assistant conductors, and soloists. They must also select music, direct weekly rehearsals, plan special programs, and work closely with the other members of the music staff of the church.

CANTOR   A cantor is a unique combination of minister, music director, teacher, and chief soloist in a synagogue. Janice Roger became a cantor because of her desire to express her love of Judaism through music. As a cantor, she is involved with music at all liturgical services for the public and in all areas of the life cycle—birth, marriage, and death.

Janice's background includes a bachelor's degree in music and a bachelor's degree in sacred music from a seminary, where she studied music for the synagogue as well as philosophy and religion. Immediately upon graduation from the seminary, Janice became a cantor for a large congregation. Her career satisfaction comes from watching young people grow and develop Jewish identities. She believes a cantor most visibly helps members of congregations by elevating their spiritual lives through music.

The requirements for becoming a cantor are not consistent throughout the Reform movement. It may or may not be necessary to have attended a seminary. The employment outlook for cantors is good because there are many more positions than there are people to fill them.

More Job Information for Music Lovers

The available possibilities of a job associated with music are much greater than most people imagine. For example, whenever music lovers hear music they should ask themselves where the music came from and who wrote, sold, marketed, or packaged the music. Then they will investigate possible jobs in such areas as background music, telephone music, the military, and piano tuning. Music lovers can also learn more about job opportunities by reading books and brochures like the following ones which detail the duties, salary range, and job qualifications for numerous positions associated with music:

Brochures

American Symphony Orchestra League. Information about careers in orchestra management. 633 E Street N.W., Washington, DC 20004

Music Educators National Conference. *Careers in Music.* 1902 Association Drive, Reston, Virginia 22091.

National Association for Music Therapy, Inc. Information about careers in music therapy. 8455 Colesville Road, Suite 930, Silver Spring, Maryland 20910

Books

Bjorneberg, Paul, compiler. *Exploring Careers in Music.* Reston, Virginia: Music Educators National Conference, 1990.

Csida, Joseph. *The Music/Record Career Handbook.* New York: Billboard Publications, 1980.

Field, Shelly. *Career Opportunities in the Music Industry.* New York: Facts on File, 1990.

Gerardi, Robert. *Opportunities in Music Careers.* Lincolnwood, Illinois: VGM Career Horizons, 1991.

Harries, Meirion and Susie. *Opera Today.* New York: St. Martin's Press, 1986.

CHAPTER FOUR

Jobs for Dance Lovers

D ancing is the earliest form of artistic expression. Paintings over 50,000 years old have been found on cave walls which show people dancing in different ceremonies. They danced when their children were born, when victory occurred on the battlefield, when rain was needed, and when evil spirits needed to be driven away. People are still dancing today. Some dance for social reasons. Ballet and modern dancers dance to tell a story. Primitive peoples still dance to call up magic powers. Many simply dance for relaxation and exercise. Whatever their reasons, dancing lets people move rhythmically. Dance in its most beautiful forms is an art which has been an inspiration for musicians and painters.

Dancing has an important role in our culture, and for this reason, there are many different jobs associated with dancing. Dance lovers do not need to be performers to find careers involved with dancing; however, a knowledge of dance is required for certain jobs. Teachers are needed at all levels, from preschool dance classes to classes for professional dancers. Choreographers are needed to design the movements that go with the music in different dances. Dance performances are enhanced by the individuals who have created the costumes, scenery, and lighting. Dance therapists work in hospitals, clinics, and other rehabilitation centers to help people regain movement. Movement analysts help people eliminate poor movement habits and get rid of muscle tension by teaching them neuromuscular reeducation techniques. Dance historians, critics, and writers are needed at libraries, dance companies, and newspapers and magazines to communicate their knowledge of dance to the public. There are even dance medicine assistants—trainers, nurses, and doctors who use their knowledge of anatomy and understanding of body movements as it relates to dance to help restore people to improved health. Without question, there are countless jobs for dance lovers. At the same time, they must realize that few of them are nine-to-five jobs, since so many are associated with performances.

Choreographers Design Dances

Choreographers create new dances and dance productions, modify or adapt existing dances, and integrate dance sections into shows. They are to dancers what the composer is to music. The choreographer is the key person in a dance company. It is the choreographer's job to know what the human body can do and to use that knowledge to teach the dancers how to move their bodies in the performance of a dance. The choreographer also works with the dance company's costume designer and lighting director to produce an integrated performance.

Most choreographers are self-taught. They learn to choreograph from their own personal dance experiences or by watching other choreographers work. Choreographers draw upon their own experiences to come up with ideas for dances. At times, the music provides the idea; at other times the movement comes first and the music is added later. Choreographers must possess more than a knowledge of dance and music. They need to understand lighting, stage dimensions, and cameras. Their job will vary from company to company. However, choreographers are usually expected to teach the company dance class, choreograph pieces for the company, rehearse the dancers, choose the dance repertoire, and select guest choreographers to work with the company. The earnings of choreographers with dance companies are specified by the Society of Stage Directors and Choreographers. Choreographers of Broadway shows receive a weekly fee, an advance, and a minimum royalty. Fees for off-Broadway productions, nonprofit productions, and stock productions vary depending upon such things as size of theater and length of engagement.

As dancing flourishes, so does the need for choreographers in dance companies; opera companies; movie, television, and video productions; theaters; and nightclub shows. New avenues are opening up for choreographers. For example, in the area of ice dancing they are helping skaters perform more exquisite patterns on the ice and in the air. Roller skating is another area in which choreographers are able to help skaters perfect their movements to the music.

Notators and Reconstructors

Ballet companies throughout the world often want to reproduce the work of a great choreographer even though the choreographer may be either dead or simply unable to come and train their dancers. Since the 1920s, it has been possible to record every movement of a ballet because a system of dance notation was developed. This system, known as Labanotation, uses special symbols to record every movement of a ballet. Special training is necessary to learn this symbol system. Many universities offer training in Labanotation.

Notators used to produce the score of a dance with pencil and a ruler. Then an autographer would handcopy the score in ink or type it. With the advent of the computer, notators are now able to use a program to record each step and the need for autographers is rapidly disappearing. Individuals who can read a completed score and teach it to dancers are called reconstructors. Most reconstructors are college professors who do the work of restaging dances as freelancers. There is a very limited demand for the specialized skills of notators and reconstructors.

Dance Kaleidoscope—A Contemporary Dance Company

When dance lovers think of working for a dance company, they may immediately think of well known companies such as New York City Ballet, American Ballet Theater, The Joffrey Ballet, San Francisco Ballet, or Alvin Ailey American Dance Theater. While these organizations will have many jobs for dance lovers, a great number of jobs can also be found with smaller companies located in almost every region of the United States. To find where some of these dance companies are located, job seekers should consult *Stern's Performing Arts Directory* at a public library.

Dance lovers in Indiana have found satisfying jobs with Dance Kaleidoscope, a contemporary dance company started in 1972. It is the only professional contemporary dance company in Indiana. The company's mission is to bring the finest in choreography from around the world to their audiences. The eight-member company presents three subscriptions series a year. When they are not on stage, they perform for school children. The company also performs nationwide on tour. Because this company is small, staff members may do several jobs which would be handled by different individuals at a larger company.

Artistic Director

David Hochoy is the artistic director of Dance Kaleidoscope and is therefore responsible for the way the company looks during a performance. He has to make sure that everything happens as scheduled and that all the elements run together smoothly to make the correct technical and artistic presentation. David also teaches the company's daily dance class, choreographs dances for the company, rehearses the dancers, chooses the company's repertoire, selects guest choreographers, and works with the lighting designer, production manager, technical director, and costume designer.

Because the company is small, David must do many other jobs. One of the most important is going out into the community to tell people about Dance Kaleidoscope. David envisioned what this company would be like and what it was going to become. He publicizes this vision with every form of media so that the vision will become a reality. David also serves as a figurehead for the company for fundraising activities.

During his high school years, David became deeply involved with the arts as he studied piano, participated in the school choir, drew and painted, was a member of theater groups, participated in some theatrical productions, and entered public speaking contests. In college, he obtained a master's degree in theater but then decided against getting a doctorate because he preferred being a performer to being a member of the academic community. Knowing that he wanted to be a dancer, David went to New York City, dance center of the United States with the greatest number of companies. For several years, his life was a combination of working as a waiter at night and taking dance classes during the day. Then he took different jobs with small dance companies in New York and worked in Toronto for a year before joining the Martha Graham Dance Theater, where he stayed for ten years. He began with the company as an ordinary dancer, became a soloist, and then a rehearsal director. As a rehearsal director, David was no longer dancing; instead, he was directing the other dancers through their rehearsals. At the same time, he was also doing his own choreography and making his own dances. He became more interested in doing these things and decided to leave the company to go to Texas Christian University. For two years, as an assistant professor, David taught modern dance techniques, composition, and dance repertoire, while choreographing student productions, counseling the students, and supervising student productions.

Today, David finds his job at Dance Kaleidoscope to be challenging and compares it to overcoming the obstacles in climbing Mt. Everest, and just as rewarding. This is the only job that David is interested in doing, even if he is on call twenty four hours a day. He usually works an eight to twelve hour day; however, the closer it gets to a performance the hours increase and it is not uncommon for him to put in sixteen hour days. In his free time, David loves to watch other dance companies. He listens to music all the time because he is always trying to find new music to use in choreographing a new number for the dance company.

Administrative Assistant and Touring Director

Suzanne Yoder manages the office of Dance Kaleidoscope. She handles the payroll, orders supplies, pays bills, books tours for the dance company, and attends conferences with video tapes of performances to interest people in booking the company. The job is really neverending, as Suzanne has the responsibility for setting up the regular season performances, ordering refreshments for concession stands, mailing season tickets. In addition, she also needs to get the tickets and flyers printed for the concert series which are held in October, March, and June. She is supposed to have a forty hour work week, but like everyone else who works for a dance company, she puts in longer hours during performances to make sure everything runs smoothly. Suzanne also works in fundraising and promotes discounts for groups larger than ten. Whenever it is possible, this dance lover likes to sit back and enjoy the company's performances.

Suzanne became an instant arts lover after winning a coloring contest in third grade and receiving a toy Easter bunny as her prize. In high school, she took art classes and was influenced by a terrific teacher to continue her studies in the arts. She received an art scholarship to Murray State University and graduated from the school with a degree in advertising. In college, she combined her interests in art and business by being a member of the advertising club and Murray Art Students. She also was in charge of public relations for her sorority.

After graduation, Suzanne took a sales job with an art supply company because it had many clients in art-related fields such as advertising, public relations, and marketing. This job worked to Suzanne's advantage because through networking she got her second job as assistant marketing director at a large mall. This job gave her excellent experience for her future work at the dance company, since she helped set up promotions in the mall, placed advertisements with newspapers and radio stations, wrote press releases, helped write the shopping center newsletter, and worked with outside vendors who in turn worked with all the individual artists who would be participating in mall arts and crafts shows. Individuals who want to work with smaller companies need to have experience in more than one area, as Suzanne did.

Director of Development

Beth Ann Holmes is the development director—the person responsible for raising money for the dance company. One way she does this is by writing grant proposals for both state and federal funds. She also tries to get corporate and individual donations. Most of the money for funding Dance Kaleidoscope comes from individual donors. Because Beth is part of a small administrative staff of only three people, she has additional responsibilities. She handles the advertising for each program, with the help of two board members. Beth also writes the newsletter that goes out to all subscribers three or four times a year and works on the development of fundraisers and special events. This "jack-of-all-trades" was even in charge of a special booth at one of the large art fairs in the city, helping make the public more aware of the dance company. Even though Beth does many different jobs, her main responsibility is to raise money for the dance company.

What types of background does an individual need for a multifaceted job like this? Beth studied journalism and Spanish in college. The journalism background was good preparation for all the writing she does in her present job. She also had several internships during her college days. One semester she was an editorial intern at the Indianapolis *Business Journal.* Although it was only an entry level reporting job, it did give her more experience in writing. She did another internship in Indiana University's Division of Continuing Studies' Office of Marketing and Promotions, where she served as a freelance author involved in the public relations side of journalism. Before coming to work for Dance Kaleidoscope, Beth worked for the Commission for Downtown Incorporated, which gave her additional experience in public relations and handling special events. Beth has always been interested in the arts. She took many fine arts classes in college, and currently spends much of her free time at the art museum and at symphony concerts. Her job as development director lets her spend the workday in close contact with the arts, which suits this lover of culture.

Costume Designer

Barry Doss is the resident freelance costume designer for Dance Kaleidoscope. He works with David Hochoy, the artistic director, to create the appropriate costume designs for each performance. Because he works with dancers, Barry must make sure that the costumes will not only have artistic value but first and foremost be functional for the dancers. Costumes are different for different types of dancing, and the designer must know exactly what is needed. For example, because in ballet there is only limited movement of the upper torso, many costumes designed for the ballerina even have metal stays, while costumes for modern dance need to be designed so that the torso is free to move.

Barry watches the choreographer work with the dancers to get a design concept. The first step is to draw sketches to turn what the director wants into two-dimensional images that will give

Barry a reference point from which he can work. The reference point gives lines and colors and actual shapes. In the artistic world, such a drawing is called a rendering.

After the costume designer and the choreographer come to an agreement on a rendering, the fabric needs to be selected. Samples are gathered and brought back to the director for approval. Once the fabric selection has been made, it must be cut or draped. Muslin is used to drape and cut the pattern out directly on the form. When the drafts methods is used, a pattern is cut and then the pattern is used to cut out the material. Barry does all of this himself. In a larger company, he would have assistants. After the garment has been constructed, it is then fitted on the dancer so that the costume designer can check that it allows freedom of movement. Alterations can be made easily at this point before the final sewing. Then the costume is ready for the final sewing, followed by the finishing work. Finishing work means adding all the trim, glitter, rhinestones, buttons, snaps, and hooks and eyes that are needed for the costume. With the finishing work complete, the costume is ready for the dancer to come in for a final fitting.

Barry holds a bachelor of arts in theater, with a double emphasis in acting performance and costume design and a minor in interior and fashion design. He attended college on an acting scholarship in theater and selected Texas Christian University in Fort Worth, Texas, the first university in the country to have a department for ballet and modern dance. Before this department was created, dancers had to study in a conservatory rather than on a university campus. In college, Barry became actively involved in ballet and costuming when he worked on the ballet *Scheherezade*. He was the assistant designer for the production, which in this case meant doing most of the accessory work, such as headpieces.

At the university, he met David Hochoy and was so impressed with his choreography in *Starry Night*, a production based on the van Gogh painting with Philip Glass music, that he offered to work for David any time he needed a costume designer. Barry got the chance to work with him at the school on *Young Apollo,* a production set to Nat King Cole's music. Barry had to design four costumes for the production—costumes for a young man and three muses. Since *Young Apollo* is a mythical piece with a modern twist, the muses had to look like goddesses—but not in the traditional sense. To achieve this difficult assignment, Barry used lots of colors.

On performance night, Barry can be found backstage if he is needed. However, he would rather be sitting out front enjoying the show and seeing how all the hours of hard work have paid off. Costumes look different in the costume studio than when they are on the dancers under the stage lights, so Barry has to make sure that when the curtain goes up on a performance everything is just as he and the director planned it.

In his free time, this culture lover enjoys going to the theater, history and art museums, and large spectacular musical touring shows like *Les Misérables.* He also enjoys shopping for antiques, going to arts and crafts shows, and attending dance performances. From all these visual experiences, he is able to gather ideas and inspirations for his own work. Barry feels that being a costume designer requires versatility. During your schooling you study costume designing for dance, theatre, films, television, and commercials before a designer chooses an area in which to specialize. He also considers himself lucky to be working full time with director David Hochoy, and believes that the Dance Kaleidoscope company will become famous.

More Jobs with Dance Companies

At one time, dance lovers would have had trouble finding jobs with dance companies outside of New York City and major cities such as Chicago and San Francisco. Now there are hundreds of small companies. Unfortunately, these companies do not have large staffs of administrators. When they first start, many just have a director, but as they win acclaim they add general managers; marketing, development, and operations staff; accountants; and other administrative support. Some companies don't hire their own staffs but obtain the management help they need from a company that offers support services to several dance or other performing arts companies. Dance lovers should also consider jobs with these firms.

Teaching Dance—The Training of Dance Lovers

Children just naturally dance; they can hardly keep their bodies still. Throughout their lives, most people continue loving to dance. Millions of dollars are spent every year for dance lessons for preschoolers learning to tap and do ballet, for high school students learning social dancing, and for adults brushing up on their ballroom dance steps or simply exercising through dance. Professional ballet dancers even take lessons or daily practice classes to stay in top physical condition. Teachers are needed to train all these eager dancers in a variety of settings, such as day care centers, nursing homes, state hospitals, public schools, dance schools, colleges, studios, conservatories, and special education programs. Your dream of teaching dance can even extend to owning your own dance studio. Job opportunities appear to be best for dance lovers seeking employment as dance teachers in private studios and schools.

Teaching dance gives dance lovers an opportunity not only to be closely involved with dance but to actually dance on the job. Do you think that you possess the necessary special skills and knowledge to be a dance teacher? Ask yourself the following questions:

1. Do you have an anatomical understanding of how the body works?

2. Do you have the ability to relate to people of different ages?

3. Do you enjoy music?

4. Do you have the ability to choreograph dances for other people?

5. Do you have the patience to teach the same step over and over?

6. Do you have the organizational skills needed to break a dance down into parts and then reteach each part until the whole dance has been mastered?

7. Do you have the skills necessary to keep discipline in a class?

8. Do you possess a sense of rhythm?

9. Are you able to express ideas, moods, and emotions through dance movements?

10. Are you self-confident?

11. Are you creative?

12. Are you able to work under pressure at times?

13. Do you have ambition?

14. Do you have talent?

15. Are you willing to spend long hours in training and practice?

16. Do you have good physical endurance?

17. Do you have leadership ability?

18. Do you have a sincere interest and love of dancing?

Dance lovers truly qualified to become dance teachers will answer "Yes" to almost every one of the above questions. To actually teach dance, the training and educational background needed will depend on the type of dance you wish to teach and where you want to teach. Many private dance teachers have trained since early childhood, and their own personal background acts as the foundation of their teaching. Most of these dancers will continue their own lessons and practice sessions even after they have started to teach dance. Dance lovers who want to teach in a public school, however, will need to have bachelor's degrees and credentials just like other teachers in the educational system. According to the American Dance Guild, the average salaries of teachers in private practice range between $11,000 and $33,000 a year, while dance teachers in schools and colleges earn between $16,500 and $35,000 a year.

This Dance Teacher Has His Own Studio

Russell Clark is the regional dance director for the Arthur Murray International Dance Organization, which has a network of 250 franchised dance studios in the United States. His duties are two-fold, as he has to train both dance instructors and dance students. Russell is also a judicator for the world professional dance teachers' organization. In this capacity, he judges dance competitions in the Midwest region comprising thirteen states, as well as international competitions.

Russell began his dance career immediately after completing high school. He took a four-week training program at the franchised studio where he was going to work. This just whetted his appetite for dance, so he started taking lessons in different areas, including tap, ballet, and jazz. Since his first lessons, he has studied and practiced every day for at least two hours. With his lessons completed, Russell began teaching in Chicago and worked with new students, giving them their first twenty lessons in ballroom dancing. He worked his way up the dance studio career ladder to become a supervisor. At this level, Russell trained all new students and was even training teachers. In this business, Russell points out, teachers need to be trained in interpersonal skills as well as in technical teaching skills, for they must help their students relax and overcome nervousness. It is also important for teachers to be able to explain in a clear way what the students need to do to accomplish their goals.

Teaching dance in a studio is definitely not a nine-to-five job. Most teachers work a 60–hour week and spend at least two to three hours additionally every day working on their own dancing. Owning a dance studio franchise as Russell now does means even more work and responsibilities; he must not only attract new students, but also needs to keep them coming back. At the present time, he is planning to add a babysitting area, which should appeal to young couples because it will let them bring their children to the studio. When you own a dance franchise, you are running a small business. You will probably need to have a lawyer and a bookkeeper. You will be keeping records, collecting fees, paying taxes, keeping track of renewal dates, following local, state, and federal business and tax laws. In addition, to keep your business going you will need to have a long-range development plan.

Russell has been successful with his dance studio franchise. He believes that interest in dancing is growing, and that people who are willing to devote enormous amounts of time and effort can have successful franchise operations. He now has two locations and six to ten employees at each location.

There is no question that Russell is a confirmed dance lover. Besides working in the field, for recreation he and his wife go out dancing at least twice a week and still perform together. Furthermore, he still enjoys dancing just as much as when he started after completing high school and was new to the dance business.

A Teacher of Ballroom, Exercise Dancing, and Ballet

Johanna Bruyn is owner of Johanna's World of Dance Incorporated. She was born in Indonesia and lived in The Netherlands before coming to the United States. As a child, she danced all the time. She had to abandon hopes for a dance career because of limited finances when her family moved to this country. Nevertheless, she never forgot her love of dance and always remembered the thrill she had turning and twirling as a young ballerina. Dance with all its joys came back into her life when she was twenty seven and started going to discos. For three years, she drove to Chicago every weekend and trained with Charles and Rosemary Mattison. The Mattisons had impressive credentials as teachers, having won the prestigious Harvest Moon Ball dance contest. They used the prize money to open a studio to train others. Many of their students have also gone on to win the Harvest Moon Ball contest.

Johanna started teaching dance at the Free University in Indianapolis in 1976, with Jim Skolburg. Their classes always had from sixty to eighty people at each session. The Free University was just getting started at this time, and the money which was made from the dance classes helped the university to take off and become a viable school in the community. Johanna also started taking lessons from her current mentors Dale Willman and Lee Harris. According to Johanna, lessons are always essential for dance teachers to keep their skills sharp and to pass on the latest steps to their students.

For almost six years Johanna operated her own studio; now she offers dance programs at clubs and community centers, and as part of adult/community education programs. She enjoys the flexibility of doing dance at different places. Johanna is such a successful teacher that she and her students have even danced the Viennese waltz in performance with the Indianapolis Symphony Orchestra. She also uses her background to teach a form of exercise workout that she invented which uses jazz. Johanna likes a more stylized form of exercise than the usual aerobics. In her workout, there is more choreography and lots of stretches and isometrics. It is a low-impact form of exercise.

Johanna does not limit her teaching to her jazz workout or ballroom dancing. After she learned the art of teaching ballet from Virginia Holte, Johanna began teaching ballet; she now teaches over 100 little ballerinas. Her preschool classes have children from $2\frac{1}{2}$ to 5 years old. Most ballet schools will not work with children this young. She gets all of her business from the word-of-mouth advertising of her satisfied students and a small ad in the yellow pages.

A Teacher of Social Dancing and Etiquette

Rebecca Kreuger Malenkos majored in English in college and became a high school English teacher, but her true love is the dancing which has always been a part of her life. She started taking dance lessons at the age of four and studied ballet, tap, jazz, and ballroom dancing for over thirteen years. In high school, she not only danced but was also in the choir and musical productions. By the time Rebecca was in tenth grade, she had become a student assistant at the ballroom dancing school for young people where she had taken lessons in social dancing and etiquette since she was in sixth grade. She gained even more teaching experience in college through teaching ballroom dancing at Wake Forest University and at a neighboring women's college. Her six-week courses for college students were a way for the students to not only learn to dance but also to meet each other in a social situation. After college, Rebecca operated her own school in Texas called Rebecca's Cotillion, where she taught dance etiquette and such basic ballroom dances as the fox trot, waltz, swing, and tango. After moving to Indianapolis, she reopened Rebecca's Cotillion. There is more than teaching dance to operating her school. Students have to receive written invitations, publicity must be done to advertise the school, and she has to solve the logistical problem of having an equal number of boys and girls for each class.

A College Professor of Dance

Stephan Laurent is the Chairman of the Department of Dance at Butler University and also an associate professor at the university. Like so many dance teachers, Stephan was a professional dancer with a long performance career before he started to teach. He didn't start studying dance until almost twenty which is rather late for a professional dancer to begin.

Stephan interrupted his performance career to study at Southern Methodist University, where he received both his bachelor's and master's degrees. He became an associate professor of dance at the University of Wisconsin-Milwaukee, leaving there to become the artistic director of the Des Moines Ballet, now known as Ballet Iowa. Stephan then chose to move to Butler University where 39 percent of the school's dance graduates go on to have a professional performing career—one of the highest number of graduates in the country to go into professional careers. In his present job, Stephan supervises the dance faculty, establishes the curriculum, and choreographs productions. Because the Butler Ballet Company is run like a professional company and puts on five or six shows a year, there is considerable choreographing for all the faculty members to do. Students also get a chance to choreograph, though the dance company is run by the faculty. Stephan explains that jobs like his at the university level require incredible dedication, energy, and physical, mental, and emotional endurance. They also allow dance lovers to be closely involved with several aspects of dancing.

Organizations for Dance Teachers

Dance lovers who are considering a career in the teaching of dance should contact dance associations for solid career information. Prospective dance teachers should also read the publications of these associations to keep abreast of what is happening in dance. And they should consider attending association conventions to meet dance teachers and watch demonstrations of the latest dance techniques.

The following dance organizations can provide helpful information to dance teachers:

American Dance Teachers Association; Vienna, VA

American Society of Russian Style Ballet; Boston, MA

Associated Dance Teachers of New Jersey; Chatham, NJ

British Dance Teachers Association; Montana, CA

Canadian Dance Teachers Association; Vancouver, BC

Ceccheti Council of America; Detroit, MI

Chicago National Association of Dance Masters; Chicago, IL

Dance Educators of America; Caldwell, NJ

Dance Masters of America, Inc.; Orlando, FL

Golden State Dance Teachers Association; Downey, CA

Imperial Society of Teachers of Dancing (U.S. Ballroom Branch); Nashua, NH

International Dance Seminars, Inc.; Long Beach, NY

Arthur Murray, Inc.; Coral Gables, FL

National Association of Dance & Affiliated Artists, Inc.; Millbrae, CA

National Council of Dance Teachers Organizations; Richmond Hill, NY

New York Society of Teachers of Dancing; Bellmore, NY

Professional Dance Teachers Association, Inc.; Waldwick, NJ

Southern Association of Dance Masters, Inc.; Lonoke, AZ

Southern Oregon Dance Association, Inc.; Oakland, OR

Texas Teachers of Dancing; Lubbock, TX

United States Dance Teachers Association; Los Angeles, CA

American Dance Guild

One dance organization which can provide valuable information to all who have or want to have careers in some aspect of dance is the American Dance Guild (ADG). The guild was founded in 1956 by a group of New York dance professionals seeking services and information in their pursuit of excellence within the field. The guild has become a multiservice organization providing a forum for the exchange of ideas and methods through its publications, conferences, and seminars. The ADG provides representation to national arts and education policy groups and an informed voice on behalf of dance to government agencies, corporations, and the public at large. This organization works to achieve Isadora Duncan's vision, "I see America dancing!"

The American Dance Guild can help dance lovers by providing:

- A newsletter which has a variety of bibliographies on dance resource books;
- A journal of American dance;
- Information about the Guild's major national conference which brings prominent professionals in dance together with ADG members and the public to share ideas;
- A forum for the exchange of ideas through conferences, publications, the Dance Resource Center, special interest groups, and seminars;
- Job information through the Job Express Registry;
- Career guidance for students and professionals in transition;
- Library access to new publications;
- A student scholarship program;
- A health insurance program;
- A speakers bureau;
- Mailing lists to dance enthusiasts.

In addition, the ADG has career information for the following dance careers:

Administration/Management	Historian
Choreography	Notator
College/University	Performer
Community Studios/Centers	Researcher
Critic/Writer	Studio
Elementary/High School	Therapist

If you want information from the ADG, send a self-addressed stamped business-sized envelope to:

American Dance Guild
  31 West 21st Street, Third Floor
  New York, New York 10010

An Employee of the American Dance Guild

Dance lovers do not have to be directly involved with dancing to have a satisfying career in the dance arena. Each of the associations has jobs which will let dance lovers be closely involved in dance. These jobs may be either full time or part time. Karen Deaver has one of these jobs as the managing director of the American Dance Guild. Her duties include coordinating programs, organizing volunteers, handling all correspondence, membership, and administration. Karen has a bachelor's degree in comparative literature, but it is her prior experience with a dance company and her own work as a dancer that qualified her for this job.

During her years in school, she danced and performed. Her first job out of school was as an administrative assistant for a modern dance company. After a promotion, she became the company manager. She has now been working for the American Dance Guild for the last three years. She started as the office manager and has risen to her present position. She works twenty five hours a week at this job so that she can continue to dance. To stay in top shape for dancing, she takes about ten hours of lessons a week. The cost of lessons can range from $7.00 to $9.00 for $1\frac{1}{2}$ hours. In one studio, she teaches in exchange for her lessons. According to Karen, working dancers need another job unless they are with a large company. Karen also performs and is a choreographer.

Dance/Movement Therapy—Better Health Through Dancing

Dance/movement therapists use movement to improve the physical and emotional health of the people with whom they are working. The American Dance Therapy Association defines dance/movement therapy as the psychotherapeutic use of movement as a process which furthers the emotional and physical integration of the individual. To become a dance/movement therapist, dance lovers need to complete both an undergraduate program with emphasis in psychology and training in a variety of dance forms, followed by professional training at the graduate level and an internship. You also need to be able to perform, choreograph, and teach dance. Dance/movement therapists need to have a strong desire to work with others and the patience, dedication, and stamina to get the job done.

The moving body is the medium of the dance/movement therapist's work. The therapist focuses on the communicative, expressive, and adaptive aspects of nonverbal behavior, using these to help clients effect changes in thinking, feelings, physical functioning, and behavior. The method consists of structuring and guiding bodily experience toward an expression of wholeness and self-awareness. This involves:

- Identification and release of psycho-emotional-physical blocks in the body, thereby increasing range of motion;
- Increasing the dynamic range of the body's movement options, or patterns;
- Providing a clear and safe context for the client to connect present bodily experience with past and present emotional traumas and/or issues;
- Facilitating a creative, imaginative, exploratory atmosphere where clients are able to discover and establish new patterns for interacting with others.

Most dance/movement therapists work in psychiatric hospitals and community health centers. Jobs are also available in hospitals, special schools, rehabilitation centers, developmental centers, correctional facilities, and nursing homes. Dance/movement therapy is a relatively new career. At the present time, these therapists do not need a state license to practice. The American Dance Therapy Association distinguishes between therapists who are prepared to work within a team or under supervision and those who can work independently. Therapists with the title Dance Therapist Registered (DTR) have a master's degree and are fully qualified to work in a professional treatment system. Therapists with the title Academy of Dance Therapists Registered (ADTR) have met additional requirements and are fully qualified to teach, provide supervision, and engage in private practice.

Dance/movement therapists work with a variety of populations, including the emotionally disturbed or physically disabled; with children, adolescents, and older people; in group and individual sessions. They can also provide valuable information to a treatment team on a client's status and behavioral patterns, make assessments, and propose movement-based interventions. Dance/movement therapy encourages the client to take an active role in her or his own process of gaining or regaining health and an optimal level of functioning.

The Work of a Dance/Movement Therapist

James Lobley, DTR is a dance/movement therapist with the Child and Family Program at the Hancock Center for Movement Arts, and Therapies, Inc. He does both individual and group movement therapy in working with children from the ages of three to twelve. James also does family therapy through dance. The type of children with whom he works includes special needs children, developmentally delayed children, children with social and emotional difficulties, and children who have been sexually abused. As a dance/movement therapist, he teaches social skills and helps children learn the proper outlet for their feelings. Dance/movement therapy uses a holistic approach in the way it perceives movement as an integral part of the whole human being. Through physical movements, dance/movement therapists are able to change people on a deeper psychological level; they can also affect how clients perceive themselves. James is currently working with a program called "Once Upon A Time," an afterschool program (K–3) using fairy tales and creative movement to address the developmental, personal, and interpersonal issues of children.

In college, James majored in French and semiotics at Brown University. After graduation, he danced for two years, while serving as an apprentice in woodworking. After a short while, he decided that he would rather work with people than inanimate objects, so he entered a two-year dance/movement therapy program at New York University. Few colleges in the United States have master's programs in dance/movement therapy. Becoming a registered dance/movement therapist is a long process involving a master's degree plus a 700–hour internship. James did his internship at a private school for language-impaired children on Long Island. Returning to Indianapolis, at a local hospital he led movement recreational activities, and gender and psychotherapy groups. He also assisted in development of treatment plans, offered individual counseling, and served as family liaison at the hospital before coming to his present job.

Movement Analyst Specialist

Idrienne Sobel-Steiman is an assistant professor at Butler University who teaches ballet dance to majors, as well as dance therapists, fitness instructors, and other college students interested in understanding and changing movement of the body. Idrienne is a certified movement analyst. Most jobs for movement analysts are found in the college setting. Idrienne teaches classes in body alignment, Laban Movement Analysis, and improvisation. In teaching these classes, she draws upon her background in three movement reeducation methods to teach the students techniques for changing poor or inefficient movement habits. She also uses these techniques to teach them how to prevent injuries and strengthen their bodies. Idrienne works mostly with ballet students. In the past ten years, the process of teaching dance has become more anatomically and scientifically based as dancers want to learn more about movement. This has resulted in a demand for college teachers, like Idrienne, who can teach the science of dance.

Idrienne's educational background includes bachelor's and master's degrees in dance. She also has taken ballet lessons since she was eight, studying at such prestigious schools of dance as Juilliard and Joffrey and spending a summer at *Le Centre de Danse International* in Cannes, France. In pursuing her original career choice of becoming a dancer, she worked with wonderful teachers like Andre Eglevskey from Russia, Melissa Hayden at Skidmore College, and her mentor Marty Morginsky who took her under his wing and helped and inspired her to develop the talent she had.

Her career path to her present job includes jobs both in the dance and business worlds. After completing her bachelor's degree, Idrienne needed to find a job and got one in arts administration at the Joffrey Ballet. This job was a full time, forty-hour-a-week job, so she danced every evening in classes taught by Finis Jhung and David Howard. Idrienne's next career move was to decide she really wanted to teach and not dance in a company. To make sure this decision was right for her, she tried the business world, working on Wall Street in commodities and then at what she calls a great job with *Vogue* Magazine, which didn't satisfy her because her heart remained with dancing.

So after working in many different fields, she went to graduate school to get her master's in dance. During this time, she was teaching dance and dance workshops and working for physical therapists using her knowledge of therapeutic exercise, as well as seeing private patients. At this point in her life, she was juggling a variety of jobs including performing with the Joffrey company when it came to California, choreographing, and even performing as a movie extra. She also began to study with body therapists in the Los Angeles area and started to understand body therapies and the relationship of the mind and the body and how the mind affects movement. With this knowledge of dance and body movement, Idrienne knew she wanted to help people become more aware of themselves through movement, help them get rid of pain through movement, and enable them to function better in their lives whether they were dancers or secretaries or accountants. If Idrienne had to describe her career in the dance world, she would explain how she has gone from being a dancer who always wanted to perform to being an educator in a new field of dance.

More Information about Dance Careers

Dance is the most fundamental of the arts, as it gives people the opportunity to directly express themselves through their bodies. Not only is dance a powerful form of expression, it is a powerful medium for therapy. The job outlook is good for dancers and culture lovers looking for jobs with regional companies or dance groups connected with colleges. With the general interest in dance increasing, the opportunities for employment in other areas aligned with dance have also increased, so dance lovers may be able to find a career niche closely associated with some aspect of dance.

You will be able to obtain additional information about colleges and universities offering degrees in dance by contacting one of the following organizations:

National Dance Association
   a Division of the American Alliance for Health, Physical
     Education, Recreation, and Dance
   1900 Association Drive
   Reston, VA 22091
   (enclose stamped, self-addressed envelope)

The American Guild of Musical Artists
   1841 Broadway, Room 911
   New York, NY 10023

American Dance Therapy Association
   Suite 108, 2000 Century Plaza
   Columbia, MD 21044

In addition, *Dance Magazine* publishes a College Guide Directory to dance in North American colleges and universities, which is available in some libraries or by contacting *Dance Magazine*, 33 West 60 Street, New York, NY 10023.

To be more knowledgeable about the career opportunities that exist in dance, dance lovers should investigate such dance-oriented publications as *Dance Magazine, Dance Teacher Now, Dance Pages, American Dance,* and *Ballet Review.*

CHAPTER FIVE

Jobs for Theater Lovers

Theater comes from the Greek work *theatron* which means a place for seeing. And theater lovers started going to performances in the Dionysus theater in Athens about 500 B.C. By 52 B.C., the first permanent stone theater was built in Rome; much later, in 1576, the first permanent English playhouse was built. The famous Globe Theater, where many of Shakespeare's plays were performed, was built in 1599. Nevertheless, for theater lovers, the word *theater* stands for far more than a building. For them, it includes all aspects of play production.

Theater is a very complex art that requires many specialists to create a production. Today, in the most sophisticated Broadway presentations, producers, directors, set designers, costume designers, lighting designers, sound designers, stagehands, and business staff are all needed to create a play. In musical productions, choreographers, conductors, and orchestras will also be required.

Where Theater Lovers Will Find Jobs

Not just in large cities but throughout the United States, groups are producing plays. Wherever plays are produced, there are jobs or opportunities to gain experience as unpaid volunteers. When theater lovers think of jobs in the theater, they may automatically think of jobs on Broadway since it has achieved so much fame from its professional theater. There are, however, many other commercial (for profit) theaters besides Broadway, although the latter generally require the largest staff. Off-Broadway theaters have smaller productions in smaller theaters and less staff than Broadway productions. Community theaters usually depend on volunteers, except for a paid director for a production. Other opportunities for jobs in commercial theater exist in stock and dinner theaters, although stock productions usually only operate on a seasonal basis. Successful Broadway productions frequently spawn national touring companies which play in major cities like Chicago, Washington, and Los Angeles. Then smaller companies are formed to tour less populous areas. In addition, some companies mount theatrical productions for industrial shows.

More people are employed in nonprofit theater than commercial theater. The greatest number of jobs is found in the theaters that are members of the League of Resident Theaters (LORT) a group of equity theaters including the American Conservatory Theater (ACT) in San Francisco, the Arena Stage in Washington, and the Actor's Theatre in Louisville, Kentucky. Other theaters in the nonprofit sector include Off-Off Broadway theaters, theaters on college campuses, and children's companies. Employment in Off-Off Broadway theaters is usually for one play, and the staff receive very low wages. Some college theaters are professional theaters with a permanent staff, while most children's theaters are small and depend greatly on volunteers unless they are members of LORT.

The Jobs Theater Lovers Want

There's no business like show business for theater lovers. They want to work in the same world legends like the Barrymores, Helen Hayes, Richard Burton, and Laurence Olivier once inhabited. Hollywood stars like Elizabeth Taylor and Lauren Bacall and television stars like Tyne Dailey and Lucille Ball have also felt this magical attraction. It is not just the stars that attract theater lovers, it is the magic of seeing plays such as *Death of a Salesman* and *A Streetcar Named Desire*. In the first days of theater, there really weren't any jobs for theater lovers: the playwright did everything, including acting. Over the years, more specialists emerged to help performers bring plays to life. What follows is a bird's eye view of some jobs in the theater. In large companies there will be many jobs for assistants and interns while in small companies individuals will handle several jobs.

Director

Directors are the interpreters of plays. They make the decisions which determine what the production as a whole will be like. This involves working with the designers of scenery, lighting, and costumes before and during the rehearsals so that each aspect of the play will reflect the planned mood or theme. Another area of responsibility for directors is selecting a cast that will give the desired performance. Directors also supervise the rehearsals and coordinate the work of everyone involved in the play to create the final product.

Directors may have collaborators, including assistant directors, stage managers, and secretaries. The stage managers are normally in charge of organizing tryouts and of the backstage during performances. The route to becoming a director can often be traced back to having been a secretary, an assistant director, and a stage manager. Another path is through an internship as an assistant director.

The Business Side of Theater

While most theater lovers may envision themselves working backstage, there are many jobs in the theater offices that must be done to keep a theater company functioning. Within this arena are the fundraisers, accountants, box office staff, publicists, marketing experts, educational program coordinators, group sales managers, and the clerical staff. And when a theatrical production goes on tour, a tour manager is needed to handle transportation and living quarters, oversee publicity and the payroll, and to deal with the presenters who are providing the facility for the play. In the commercial theater, a producer is needed to find the money for a play and hire the staff to produce it. Many theater lovers can enjoy a career within the business confines of the theatrical world.

Director of Marketing

The responsibilities of marketing directors will vary because of the different needs of theater companies. James Habegger, director of marketing at the Indianapolis Civic Theatre, is in charge of group sales, direct publicity, and advertising. In the community theater where James works, there are four people who act as the marketing team to promote the theater with the public. They are the executive director of the theater, the director of marketing, the director of development, and the director of publicity. Teamwork is the key at the Civic Theatre. When James has a good radio or television spot and the director of development has a good corporate sponsor, they will work to bring these two elements together.

James' college background is in performance arts and music. His interest in the theater can be traced back to high school and college performances in musicals. After graduation from college, James pursued his musical interests by performing at Bear Creek Farms, a 100–seat theater, as part of a group that put on musical reviews. James' next job was at a dinner theater in North Carolina where he performed in five shows a week and made $35 a show. To earn living expenses, he worked as a maintenance man in a hotel. After a year in show business, James went to work with an insurance company because he simply couldn't make enough money in the theater. His job consisted of answering angry phone calls eight hours a day which he feels was good training for working with the public, as he does in his current job. James had just started taking marketing classes when he obtained his present job, where he feels that he is constantly learning more about marketing every day. James still enjoys performing in musicals; however, since he spends eight to ten hours daily at the Civic Theatre, he prefers to perform at another theater, since returning to his theater is like going back to work. This avid theater lover can't seem to get enough of the theater in Indianapolis so he also goes to theatrical productions in Chicago and New York.

Director of Development

Directors of Development are fundraisers. Katharine Lange procures money for the Civic Theatre from individuals, corporations, and governmental entities. Part of her job consists of cultivating an awareness with potential donors of what the Civic Theatre is and what it does. She describes herself as a "one-man band" fundraising organization.

Katharine brings excellent credentials to her job as director of development. She holds a master's degree in arts administration, specializing in the areas of fundraising and public relations. This degree is a relatively new one; however, it serves as excellent academic preparation for those wishing to work on the business side of the theater. Katharine gained more expertise in working for theaters through her internship as a public relations associate at the Arena Stage in Washington, D.C. where she did a variety of things including press relations, research on the background of the productions, editing for the theater program, press writing, media hosting, and handling requests for press releases and photo shoots. Because Arena Stage is located in the nation's capital, she often had to give theater tours to visiting dignitaries. After completing her internship, she returned to Indianapolis and worked in the marketing department at a bank before taking her present job, which ties in with her lifetime interest in theater.

Today, as Director of Development for a community theater, Katharine believes that the arts are currently in trouble because of reduced contributions from the government and because several major corporations in her town have disappeared after being taken over by other companies. This is why she is constantly seeking new sources to fund the Civic Theatre.

Volunteer Coordinator

Adrienne Reiswerg grew up in New York City, close to Broadway. She went to many shows with her family and developed a love of the theater when she was quite young. Adrienne has continued this family tradition by taking her sons to the theater in Indianapolis. In school, camp, and college, she was involved in dramatics. Adrienne's college training was in education, and she taught elementary school for five years. On returning to the work arena after starting a family, she obtained a job working for the Riley Hospital Telethon as a volunteer coordinator. The job of recruiting volunteers and designing volunteer projects had flexible work hours, involved some travel, and gave her the opportunity to work with different groups. She left this job to enjoy raising her family, acting in community theater, and serving as a volunteer at the Civic Theatre.

While Adrienne was a volunteer, money became available at the Civic Theatre to hire a person to match interested volunteers with programs needing personnel, to expand the volunteer program, and to create new projects. The sum available for this position was only sufficient to fund a part time job, which was ideal for Adrienne. She currently works 19 hours a week as the volunteer coordinator, with some weekend and evening hours.

Adrienne got her job through her activities as a volunteer because she was in the right place at the right time and because she was able to accept part time work. Prerequisites for this job include the ability to speak in public, write clearly, and organize and execute projects. In this field, you should also like to work with people. While a theater or college degree is not essential for her job, most theater companies tend to hire individuals with degrees.

Adrienne enjoys her job because she works with wonderful people, while making a contribution to the theater. She also finds it satisfying to know that she is part of an organization that brings beauty and recreation to so many—in addition to being thought provoking. At the present time, the position of volunteer coordinator is extremely important to community theaters, since limited budgets are forcing them to turn to volunteers to do many jobs.

Because Adrienne is only a part time employee, her benefits are not the same as those of full time employees who have health and insurance benefits. However, she enjoys the benefits of flexible hours. And believe it or not this theater lover spends part of her free time doing volunteer work at other theaters.

The Technical Side of Theater

Costume Designer

Clare Gee became interested in theater during high school. Because her school was small, she became involved in every aspect of the theater when she participated in plays—from acting to set building. Bitten by the theater bug, she planned to major in English and minor in theater at college. However, after two years of college she changed her major to science and became a science teacher.

Working as a freelance seamstress gave Clare the opportunity to learn sewing techniques. Her introduction to the world of costume design came when she volunteered to sew for a theater. Through this activity, she learned costuming skills which she put to work with her theater background. Then she became a freelance costume designer, making costumes for local theaters. The next step was a position as costume supervisor at the Christian Repertory Theater, where she now works four or five hours a day and enjoys a flexible schedule. After making costumes for one show at the theater, she was asked to organize and operate the costume shop.

Clare uses her educational background, especially her history courses, when she is doing research to determine what type of costumes would be appropriate for a play. She especially enjoys the study and research and then moving on to a new and different project. She picked up her sewing skills through personal practice and has taken art courses to improve her sketching.

As Clare has demonstrated, it is not difficult to get into the costume design department at a community theater as a volunteer. However, to be paid for this work you must demonstrate that you are efficient, can be creative with the allotted budget, and produce good design work. In the future, she is considering a career in costume design in television or movies, which pay better than theater, but she is undecided about this. She still loves theater.

The Set Designer

Sets aren't just pretty backgrounds for theatrical productions. They are the environment where the action takes place. Sets add to actors' characterizations as well. If the curtain goes up on a messy room with papers all over the floor, you get a different impression of the character who lives in this room than if the room were absolutely spotless. Sets also tell the audience about the time and place a play is portraying—such as colonial or Victorian, in New England or in Mexico. Audiences can also expect the set to define the mood of a play. Successful sets increase an audience's understanding of a play.

SET DESIGNER AT AMERICAN REPERTORY COMPANY (ACT)   Joel Fontaine is in an unusual position as resident set designer for ACT, since most set designers are freelancers. Joel's work in designing the set for a play begins when he reads the play a couple of months before rehearsals for the play are to start. If he were freelancing, Joel would also visit the theater at this time so he could make his design fit the theater. After reading the play, the next step for set designers is a meeting with the director to discuss what the play means. Joel may bring pictures to this meeting to show what he thinks the look or the mood of the play is. If Joel and the director have worked together previously, the first meetings are smoother. At the next meeting with the director, Joel will have rough sketches or a model. The director's reaction can range from loving to hating Joel's initial ideas. However, over the course of three or more meetings with the director, Joel will refine his sketches until the two have agreed on a working model which is done to scale.

At this point, the producer of the play may also be consulted for his approval. Joel then makes a finished model—with every detail complete, from paint to furniture to molding on the door. A few designers have help from assistants in constructing the finished model. Joel then shows the director the completed model as a final step in the design process.

Joel does not draw the construction details when he works at ACT. Instead, an ACT shop draftsperson will do this. While the set is being built at the ACT shop, Joel may check on it. Once the set is built, it goes to the paint shop. At times, Joel has to give the scene painter a flat rendering of the set if the painting of the set is to be quite complex. During the time the set is being built, Joel must confer with the lighting, prop, and costume designers. He wants to make sure that all of these elements will blend with his design. He certainly doesn't want an actress to be wearing a plaid outfit that is the same design as the upholstery on the couch. When he freelances, Joel may have to draw the construction details, paint the set, and get the props.

Joel will go to a play rehearsal and show the actors the model of the set and will check at this time to ensure that the actors aren't walking through places on the stage that will be walls. Approximately a week to ten days before the play opens, the scenery is taken to the theater. Now is the time the set designer checks that everything works as it should. The lighting and sound designers now come to work on the set. Joel will be at the technical rehearsal while all the lighting and sound problems are solved. The actors wear their costumes at the dress rehearsal, and changes are still being made so everything works together—scenery, lighting, clothes, paint.

Joel began his career in New York city assisting other designers and doing design work himself, after completing a master's program in set design at Yale. Joel is a set designer in the theater simply because he can't imagine doing anything else. The two major frustrations of his career as a freelancer are low wages and always having to be looking for his next job.

DESIGN ASSOCIATE   At the ACT, Joel has a design associate, Dawn Swiderski. She does many of the tasks Joel would have to do when he freelances. Because ACT's theater was destroyed in the last serious San Francisco earthquake, Dawn will go out to measure the visiting stage ACT is using for a play before Joel begins designing the set. When Joel has completed the set design, she will do the construction drawings for the scene shop. She will then serve as the liaison between the set designer and the shop. She also has to work closely with the scene painter. At all times, she must make sure that everyone in the carpentry shop and paint shop have all needed information. Dawn was already familiar with set design before she came to the ACT, as she had assisted professional set designers when she was in college studying for her bachelor's degree in theater design and production. After college, she got a design internship at ACT and became an associate designer when her predecessor left.

Set Builder

After the designer and the director have agreed on the design of a set, the designer or an assistant makes a detailed set of drawings which shows every detail of the construction. Large theater organizations will have their own shops or use independent firms that specialize in building sets. In the case of nonprofessional companies, the set designer and a volunteer crew may do all the construction using the stage as their shop. ACT has its own shop which also builds sets for other stage shows in San Francisco and throughout the country.

Ed Raymond is the scene shop foreman of the ACT shop and the technical supervisor of the ACT company. As shop foreman, he supervises a core crew of four or five plus a scene painter. Depending on the time allotted for a job, the complexity of the set design and the money available, Ed's crew may expand to as many as twenty people. Everyone working on the crew, including Ed, is a member of the union. When Ed needs to hire additional crew, he hires union people who can do the job. The union has an apprentice stagehand program to train stagehands for working in the theater, movies, and television. Apprentices gain experience by scene shop work, lectures, and reading material for self-study. In addition to the union crew, Ed usually has two interns who are just out of college, working for a very small amount of money to get exposure to set building and designing.

There is not much turnover in Ed's crew because they truly enjoy this work. Jobseekers who get crew jobs usually have had experience building scenery in college or elsewhere. It must be pointed out that these jobs, including Ed's, are seasonal. The crew only works when there is a job to do. For Ed, this usually means approximately eight months a year. Only a few scene shops will employ crew full time.

In his role as shop foreman, Ed may find himself covered with sawdust as he works with his crew to build the set. They must frequently consult the blueprints to make sure the set is being built precisely as the set designer envisioned. The designer will have consulted with Ed during the design process to ensure that design ideas can be built within the budget allowed and that the set as designed can be constructed as a light and portable unit. Ed's job as shop foreman includes deciding which materials will be needed for each job and then ordering them. He also must make sure that all of the work is done within the limits of the budget. In addition to building the set, Ed's crew is responsible for constructing all the mechanical effects—the elevators, cranes, and winches—used in a show.

When a set is built, Ed's job as technical supervisor begins. In that capacity, he coordinates taking the set to the theater with what is actually happening at the theater. While at the theater, as well as in the shop, he works directly under the production manager. He will stay on the set during rehearsal to make sure everything about the set is functioning as planned. When the production has finished its run, Ed is in charge of removing the set. Since each set is unique, few sets are stored. Instead, only the recyclable elements are saved.

Ed never planned to work at building scenery, even though he possessed considerable skills developed from using the excellent shop in his family's home. He graduated from college with a degree in English literature and taught in elementary school, high school, and college for a while. Then a friend who was an assistant foreman in the shop at ACT told Ed about his work, and Ed was intrigued enough with the job description to start as a shop general, the lowest position in the shop. His job was basically to keep the shop clean.

Ed then became a shop mechanic. This is the job title for those who read the blueprints and assemble the sets. After a stint as assistant foreman, Ed changed his job milieu and went to work as an assistant stage carpenter. In this job, he was responsible for putting up the set when it was delivered to the theater. At this particular theater, he might have to put up the sets for two shows in one day. This was a full time job with 75 to 80 hour weeks. During that time, he also toured with ACT as a property master in charge of the show's props. Then he returned to the ACT scene shop as foreman—his present job. When Ed is not working at ACT, he works for a film company, Lucasarts, as a foreman and as a construction coordinator. This job is very similar to what he does at ACT except that the sets, crews, and budgets are bigger.

Lighting Designer

Derek Duarte is the lighting designer for ACT, in charge of all the lighting for all the plays. He must organize the technical elements as well as the artistic design. His job starts at the beginning of rehearsals and lasts to opening night, when an electrician takes over running the lights for the actual performances. By the time the curtain goes up on opening night, all the instructions for running the lights have been put in the computer.

Derek starts his work with four bare walls, a blank canvas on which to create all the lighting effects. For example, if the director says that a scene will take place on a stormy, hot night, Derek will have to create this night with the lighting designs he selects. Like the set and costume designers, he must read the play and meet with the director, as well as the other designers. Set designers and costume designers can make drawings or have fittings before the start of rehearsals, but it is a different story for lighting designers who can make schematic drawings but cannot really put the finishing touches on their work until load-in time. This is the time when everything is brought to the theater and rehearsals on the stage begin. During this time, Derek will put in extended hours, working six days a week, from eight to midnight. Eighty percent of lighting designers' work is preproduction planning. The rest of their work is done after the scenery arrives.

Being a lighting designer is an exciting, high pressure job, but Derek finds it fascinating each time he sees what he has created. Derek has been working in the lighting industry for the last eleven years. He even freelances, doing the lighting design for approximately twenty-six shows a year.

Derek has known since he was sixteen years old that he wanted to work in the theater. He always knew that he did not want to be on the stage as a performer, so he looked through a theater program for all the jobs listed for a theatrical production; he decided that being a lighting designer was the job for him. After attending a community college, he got his bachelor's degree in dramatic arts from the University of California at Berkeley. While he was at the community college, he participated in a work study program, getting minimum wage for being a stagehand. At college he worked at the renowned Berkeley Repertory Theater, a wonderful experience because the performers were from around the world. Derek obtained a master's degree in fine arts in lighting design from the University of California at Los Angeles. During his graduate studies, he was a teaching assistant and ran a lab on constructing scenery. All of Derek's jobs during his college days augmented his classroom instruction while paying for his schooling.

After graduation, Derek took numerous small jobs in the performing arts. He really never lived anywhere, but instead traveled from job to job, living in New York, San Francisco, and Los Angeles. There is considerable travel involved in being a costume, set, or lighting designer, as you have to go to where the jobs are. Returning to the San Francisco Bay Area, Derek took a job teaching lighting design for one year at Cal Berkeley, replacing someone on sabbatical. Since then he has kept the Bay Area as his home and worked for community theaters around the country. In his free time, just like every other theater lover, Derek enjoys going to the theater; however, it usually takes him ten minutes to relax and settle in to enjoy the show. During those first ten minutes, he is busing checking out the set's scenery and lighting.

Sound Designer

Sound designers produce the program sound which includes both sound effects and sound reinforcement. To make the ideal contribution to the production, the sound designer has to make the sound an integrated part of the production. Sound includes music, noises of no recognizable origin, realistic sounds such as doorbells and thunder, and any sound that is mechanically produced. In the theater, sounds that are produced electrically are considered to be part of the stage lighting.

The sound designer helps set the play's mood and enhance the story through sounds like gunshots, off-stage screams, and screeching brakes. Sounds can either be live and created for each production, or prerecorded. The sound designer holds the same type of discussions as the costume, set, and light designers do with the director. Only this time the discussion is about what should be heard during the play. Sound designers will select sounds and play them to the director for approval. Once the sounds have been approved, the sound designer will make a list of the equipment to be used and where it is to be placed. Like the lighting director, much of the work will be done after the load-in. The sound director will also be concerned with enhancing the sound of the actors and the orchestra, if there is one.

Maintenance Worker

Although Ingrid Nelson has a degree in music education, she is not working in the music arena in the theater but instead as a maintenance worker at the Civic Theatre. A friend started a cleaning business, and Ingrid became a partner and then owner of her own housecleaning firm. Just when her cleaning load had become too heavy, she saw an ad in the newspaper for a full time maintenance worker at the Civic Theatre. She was hired because of her background with her own cleaning firm and because she is well organized, efficient, and strong enough to move furniture and other set-ups. Maintenance and housekeeping in the arts does not offer a wide variety of jobs, but if an opening does arise those with no background in theater can apply and work for minimum wage. Ingrid is hoping to become the head housekeeper or maintenance supervisor and then see if she can find a job doing this work with a larger theater company.

Important Facts about Theater Jobs

Individuals considering a career working behind the scenes in the theater should realize that jobs in the performing arts are not usually permanent, except for jobs of an administrative or clerical nature. Jobs such as director and costume, set, and lighting designers usually begin and end with a show, unless one is working for a LORT theater. People take jobs in the theater because they love the surroundings. Many individuals working in the theater also hold outside jobs to earn more money because jobs in the theater do not offer high wages or job security. Even though Derek has worked at ACT for six years as a lighting designer, he is also teaching at a community college. He tells his theater students that most of them will be working at another job but will find every moment they work in the theater a joy.

Searching for a Job in the Theater

Many people currently working in the theater found their first jobs after working as an intern or a volunteer with a theater. Networking is another way to find out about jobs. In addition, the following newspapers and periodicals have job information for theater lovers:

Newspapers

Back Stage (weekly)
 165 West 46th Street
 New York, NY 10036

Show Business (weekly)
 136 West 44th Street
 New York, NY 10036

Variety (weekly)
　154 West 46th Street
　New York, NY 10036

Daily Variety
　1400 N. Cahuenga Boulevard
　Hollywood, CA 90028

Casting Call (weekly)
　3365 Cahuenga Boulevard West
　Los Angeles, CA 90068

Los Angeles Weekly
　5325 Sunset Boulevard
　Los Angeles, CA 90027

Magazines

Theatre Crafts (10 issues per year)
　135 5th Avenue
　New York, NY 10010

Theatre Design and Technology (quarterly)
　330 West 42nd Street
　New York, NY 10036

Lighting Dimensions (7 issues per year)
　31706 South Coast Highway, Suite 302
　South Laguna, CA 92677

CHAPTER SIX

More Jobs for Culture Lovers

W hen people think of culture, some may think of just art, music, dance, and the theater. This is a rather narrow definition, since the cultural world also includes literature, architecture, photography, furniture, textiles, and jewelry. As the list of arts and culture expands, so does the list of possible jobs for culture lovers. There are certainly jobs in museums, galleries, corporations, and stores for culture lovers with these interests. The list of possible jobs keeps increasing when you consider all the jobs that deal with more than one art form. Government agencies, foundations, and concert halls offer enticing opportunities for the culture lovers who want to work with several arts.

Be creative in searching for your perfect job in the arts. Investigate the possibilities by reading the want ads in your field of interest. Many of the culture lovers described in this book found their jobs in this way. Don't shun the lowest job on the career ladder in your field of interest, since it will acquaint you with the existence of more jobs in this area than you probably ever imagined. And remember that many of the culture lovers in this book found jobs by serving as interns or volunteers. Culture lovers should also search for jobs by such traditional routes as school placement offices; city, state, and federal employment offices; and private employment agencies. Here are just a few more places where art lovers can find jobs.

Unique Stores that Cater to Culture Lovers

There are stores that specialize in the selling of fine arts objects and very elegant objects for the home. Some of these stores are world famous, like Gump's in San Francisco. These stores do not just exist in metropolitan areas. Within many communities, there are stores which seem almost like museums—places in which to browse rather than to shop. They are intriguing places for culture lovers to work, especially if they are interested in several forms of arts. Culture lovers may find it especially appealing to work as salespersons and buyers in these stores.

WORKING AT A VERY SPECIAL STORE   Ron Schwarz's office at Gump's in a culture lover's delight. Oriental scrolls hang on the walls, and sculpture abounds. Nevertheless, his desk is stacked with papers attesting to the fact that there is considerable paperwork in his jobs as divisional merchandise manager for the third floor and director of interior design. As part of these jobs, he buys all the lamps, furniture, and Asian art sold in the store. This involves seeing sales representatives in his office, going to shows and furniture markets, and traveling to such cities as New York, Paris, and Milan. These buying trips are not artistic flings, since he has a budget which limits what he can purchase. An important job requirement for buyers is to have a business sense. In addition, Ron points out that successful buyers must go beyond their personal taste and choose items that will appeal to the commercial market.

Ron's jobs carry many responsibilities. He helps create the room settings on the third floor and supervises the look of the floor. He coordinates the colors used in the store. Time is spent supervising personnel and hiring new sales associates and interior designers. For both of these positions, he is more inclined to look at a jobseeker's background than at the individual's degrees. Because of the uniqueness of Gump's furnishings, clients from around the world seek the services of the design staff. Ron must spend time matching the clients to the appropriate designers.

Ron brings both a background in art and experience in the retail and design worlds to his current job. Although he majored in art in college, he believes that his knowledge of the arts with which he deals comes mainly from constant reading, studying, looking, and museum-going. Culture lovers aspiring to positions like Ron's must have this attribute of always wanting to know more. In addition, they need to have a background of varied experiences.

After the army, Ron's first job was designing a line of furniture for an importer, followed by a job working for an antique dealer and then briefly owning his own interior design studio. A part time Christmas sales job at Tiffany's led to a position as an assistant glass buyer in only six months, and later to actually designing and buying china. In 1966, Ron opened his own store in San Francisco, where he sold such objects as china, glass, and silver, and worked as an interior designer doing primarily residential work. After he closed his store to concentrate on interior design, he was asked to work at Gump's in his present position, which lets him use all of his prior experiences.

Antique Shops Deal in Valuable Art Objects

Many people tend to think of antiques as old household articles; however, other objects should be included in this category, such as coins, books, guns, toys, and even clothing. It isn't just age, however, that makes an object an antique. An object can be valued for the skill of its craftsman or because it is rare. Lovers of antiques can find jobs working with antiques as shop owners, salespersons, appraisers, auctioneers, restorers, and repairers.

And there is no shortage of antique shops in which antique lovers can work. Large cities will have hundreds of shops, while even the smallest community may have a shop, especially if the area attracts tourists.

OWNING AN ANTIQUE SHOP   For many antique lovers, a lifelong dream is to have their own antique shop to sell their favorite types of antiques. You will find shops specializing in oriental porcelains and accessories, seventeenth century French furniture, nautical antiques, brass lamps, and whatever antique shop owners fancy. John Drum has owned his own antique shop specializing in eighteenth and nineteenth century decorative furniture for the past ten years. He has one salesperson. When hiring employees John looks for people who know the basic facts about antiques and are super sales people. He believes that successful antique dealers not only must have an eye for what will sell but must also have good business skills.

John learned about antiques by growing up in a home furnished with eighteenth century English and French furniture and other antiques which his family had inherited. He studied marketing in college and worked in business for several years. After the death of his father, he decided to set up a very small antique shop with the possessions he had inherited. Before he opened the shop, he took a three-month course in London at the Study Center for the Decorative Arts. Subsequently, John learned about buying antiques when he went to Europe with a friend who taught him how to restock his shop. Today, he will make two trips to Europe a year, mostly to France. Over the years, he has established a network of shops to visit, but John is always trying to find new shops. Trip abroad are not restful. Days are often twelve to fourteen hours long and distances covered can be great. On one trip, he covered 3000 kilometers in five days. He may just double park in front of a shop and run in and see if they have anything he is looking for. John also shops locally and attends auctions to restock his shop. Restocking an antique shop is a major job for every antique dealer.

Besides restocking his shop, John has many other tasks. He must spend time in his shop, selling antiques and seeing that the antiques which he has purchased are repaired or restored if necessary. He will usually hire others to do repair and restoration work. Time must also be spent visiting other shops and studying catalogs in order to price his antiques appropriately. Before new articles can go on the sales floor, he must write up a description of the article for the sales tag and price the piece. In addition, like most other antique shop owners he will take furniture to shows to sell it.

Books Can Be Works of Art

In the middle ages, monks would sit at their desks in monasteries painstakingly copying books which were truly beautiful to behold. Today, there are calligraphers, paper and print makers, typographers, book binders, and printers making books in artistic ways. These publishers often combine literature and art in a significant manner. A few just print visual art with text. The material published by these companies do not have mass appeal. They are rarely sold in bookstores, except rare and antiquarian stores.

There are no large publishers printing these books. Some are just individuals with tabletop presses wishing to make outstanding books of their grandmother's poetry or a buddy's Vietnam War experiences. Others are printshops with five or six employees. Only a few fine print publishers make money; most are just self-supporting.

Throughout the country, organizations exist for those interested in publishing fine books. One of those organizations is Pro Arte Libri (For the Art of Books) which has a magazine, *Fine Print*, providing news about projects, workshops, exhibitions of these books, and printing techniques. Information about this organization can be obtained by writing:

Pro Arte Libri
   P.O. Box 193394
   San Francisco, California 94119

Libraries and colleges often have book arts programs where people can learn printing, typography, and other skills essential to publishing. More information about this field can be obtained from:

The Guild of Book Workers
521 Fifth Avenue
New York, New York 10175

PUBLISHING COMPANIES   Book lovers can be actively involved in the publishing of literary works at many publishing companies. Editors work closely with the authors of fine literature in the preparation of the manuscripts of these books.

ANTIQUARIAN AND RARE BOOKSTORES   Book lovers do not have to print their own books to be associated with extraordinary books. A few bookstores just deal in antiquarian and rare books, giving book lovers the opportunity to own or work in a store buying or selling these books.

Performing Arts Centers Need Staffs

For the culture lovers who wish to be involved with opera companies, symphony orchestras, ballet companies, theater and choral groups, working as part of the staff at a performing arts center provides this opportunity. The size of the hall greatly determines the size and functions of the staff. The three largest performing arts centers are Lincoln Center in New York City, The Los Angeles Music Center, and the Kennedy Center in Washington, D.C. These centers have a large permanent staff with dozens of administrative and technical positions, as do many large universities with performing arts centers. Community performing arts centers, on the other hand, may be operated entirely by volunteers. However, these centers are excellent places for volunteers to get the experience which may lead to a full time paid position with another center.

STAFF MEMBER AT CLOWES HALL   On the campus of Butler University, Clowes Hall is one place in Indianapolis where opera, ballet, musical, and theatrical productions are presented. While Clowes Hall is decidedly not as large as the three largest performing arts centers, it would be typical for a center this size to have a permanent staff including a general manager, business manager, development director, marketing director, public relations director, and operations director, plus all of the administrative and technical staff to support these positions. Anna Thompson is the education coordinator at Clowes Hall—a newly created position. In this job, she acts as liaison with the hall's resident opera and ballet companies and local educators. She also designs participatory workshops for teachers, based on the Kennedy Center model, and schedules matinee performances for school children. In addition, she arranges for preconcert lectures for the general audience. Whatever Anna does is designed to help audiences know more about the arts and the shows presented at Clowes.

Corporations Have Jobs for Arts Lovers

Many businesses have art, archives, and artifacts of historical importance which need to be preserved, organized, and shared with the public. Researching, managing, and displaying these resources are inviting jobs for culture lovers. The number of jobs in this area, while not large, may still be greater than you imagine. For example, the Wells Fargo Bank in California has nineteen employees working in the history department of the bank under the direction of Andy Anderson, a vice president. The bank's collection of art and artifacts dates back to the Gold Rush days in California and is displayed in bank museums in four separate locations in the state and in the corporate offices. Each museum has articles which are appropriate to that area's history and presents educational programs to school children. The most visible artifacts of the bank are the fourteen stage coaches. They are seen in the museums, as well as in parades and civic events. Culture lovers working in this department of the bank even include stagecoach drivers. This department also manages the corporate archives which contain information about the development of the western frontier, since Wells Fargo is the oldest bank involved in financing in the West. According to Andy Anderson, culture lovers who would like to work in this type of corporate setting should have backgrounds in art, history, or education. Beside having bachelor's degrees, several of the employees in his department have advanced degrees.

CORPORATE GIVING JOBS   Watch a symphony or an opera on PBS, and quite often you will see the name of a corporation as the sponsor of the program. More and more corporations are associating their companies with the arts by sponsoring festivals, television programs, and touring companies. Some companies that are involved in giving to the arts have special giving departments. While there are a very limited number of jobs in this area, they are very appealing to culture lovers. Applicants with business experience are often corporations' first choice for these positions.

Arts Lovers Can Find Jobs with the Government

In Europe, it has always been traditional for state and city governments to support the arts. Not until 1965 and the creation of the National Endowment for the Arts did the United States government really begin to contribute to the arts. The mission of the National Endowment for the Arts is:

- to foster the excellence, diversity and vitality of the arts in the United States; and
- to help broaden the availability and appreciation of such excellence, diversity, and vitality.

Culture lovers reading this mission statement can readily appreciate that within this independent agency of the federal government, there are many jobs for those who wish to be a part of implementing this mission. Block grants from the Endowment's program funds are allocated to state and regional art agencies, thereby creating additional jobs for culture lovers at lower levels. In addition, even the smallest communities now have local arts commissions which can be independent or supported by the state or local government.

The individual states vary considerably in how they meet the artistic needs of their citizens. The decisions about which groups and individuals in each state will receive money to support their artistic endeavors are made by commissions appointed by the governors. The staff of the state art agencies, or councils as they may be called, usually makes recommendations to these commissions. Culture lovers with state agencies do such diverse jobs as develop arts festivals, work with the schools, help grant seekers complete their forms, and write informational books and pamphlets. The typical state art agency has an executive director, a fiscal officer, an information officer, programs directors, and a grants administrator, plus administrative and clerical support staff.

At the state level job qualifications are very specific for each open position. For example, an applicant wishing to work as a music program director would have to have a background in music. Beyond having specific skills, applicants should have these additional skills:

- a knowledge of accounting and budgeting so they can read and understand the agency's budget;
- an understanding of the importance of teamwork;
- the ability to work with volunteers;
- experience working on cultural activities, such as festivals and art shows.

Culture lovers wanting to find positions with the government in administering arts programs should look at *Job Bank* and

Artresearch. These two publications list jobs in this area and are usually found in college and public libraries and in city and state art agencies. Positions with state art agencies may or may not be civil service jobs. Entry level positions usually pay college graduates in the low $20,000 range, while individuals who have top jobs like executive directors can expect to make between $35,000 and $50,000.

The procedure for getting a job with the federal government is complicated and often takes considerable time. The best way to understand this process is by reading a book like one of the following which explains the steps you need to take:

Find a Federal Job Fast!
　　Ronald L. Krannich and Caryl Rae Krannich
　　Impact Publications
　　Woodbridge, Virginia

Guide to Federal Jobs—Second Edition
　　Editor in Chief: Rod W. Durgin
　　Resource Directories
　　Toledo, Ohio

How to Get a Federal Job
　　David E. Waelde
　　Fedhelp Publications
　　P.O. Box 15204, Dept. GOF
　　Washington, D.C. 20003

Foundations Support the Arts

The J. Paul Getty Trust is a foundation which operates seven entities in the visual arts and related humanities, including the J. Paul Getty Museum and the Getty Center for the History of Art and the Humanities. Culture lovers interested in working for organizations that provide financial support to different arts groups can have gratifying careers working in foundations. Unfortunately, there is considerable competition for these jobs, and many are obtained by word-of-mouth or networking.

Foundations are incorporated nonprofit organizations that operate by giving grants to organizations, by operating their own programs, or by a combination of awarding grants and running their own programs. Foundations are established by individuals, families, and corporations who state the purpose of the organization in the foundations' by-laws. Some foundations are concerned solely with the arts, but many have broader interests. Small foundations may not have any paid staff or may be administered by a part time director. Large foundations will have departmentalized staffs. The larger a foundation is, the better staff members are paid.

Culture lovers who are interested in working at a foundation should look at the *Foundation Directory* to determine which foundations support the arts, whether they employ a professional staff, and how large the staff is. This directory, published by The Foundation Center, can be found in public libraries and in the reference collections operated by The Foundation Center in New York City, San Francisco, Washington, D.C., and Cleveland. In addition, culture lovers should read the chapters on recruitment and career paths in *Working in Foundations*, also published by the Foundation Center, for helpful information on careers with foundations.

Volunteers and Interns Find Jobs in the Arts

A great number of culture lovers, just like you, dream of finding jobs related to art, music, dance, theater, and other fine arts. The competition for even entry level positions can be fierce in certain areas. Imagine having to have a doctorate to get certain jobs at the Smithsonian. Furthermore, many positions, especially in museums, require successful applicants to have master's degrees.

Having the appropriate academic background is still not sufficient for many jobs which are extremely competitive. The edge to getting a job is often having experience, and two of the best ways to gain this experience are by serving as a volunteer or working as an intern. Volunteers and interns learn how arts organizations operate. They can discover interesting career possibilities which they never knew existed. And they can perform so well in their jobs that they are offered positions where they have been volunteering or interning.

Arts Careers Are Immensely Gratifying

Working in careers in the arts raises the career satisfaction of culture lovers, because they are refreshed from working each day with the arts.

"The finest works of art are precious, among other reasons, because they make it possible for us to know, if only imperfectly and for a while, what it actually feels like to think subtly and feel nobly."

ALDOUS HUXLEY: ENDS AND MEANS XII

VGM CAREER BOOKS

OPPORTUNITIES IN
*Available in both paperback and
hardbound editions*
Accounting Careers
Acting Careers
Advertising Careers
Aerospace Careers
Agriculture Careers
Airline Careers
Animal and Pet Care
Appraising Valuation Science
Architecture
Automotive Service
Banking
Beauty Culture
Biological Sciences
Biotechnology Careers
Book Publishing Careers
Broadcasting Careers
Building Construction Trades
Business Communication Careers
Business Management
Cable Television
Carpentry Careers
Chemical Engineering
Chemistry Careers
Child Care Careers
Chiropractic Health Care
Civil Engineering Careers
Commercial Art and Graphic Design
Computer Aided Design and
   Computer Aided Mfg.
Computer Maintenance Careers
Computer Science Careers
Counseling & Development
Crafts Careers
Culinary Careers
Dance
Data Processing Careers
Dental Care
Drafting Careers
Electrical Trades
Electronic and Electrical Engineering
Electronics Careers
Energy Careers
Engineering Careers
Engineering Technology Careers
Environmental Careers
Eye Care Careers
Fashion Careers
Fast Food Careers
Federal Government Careers
Film Careers
Financial Careers
Fire Protection Services
Fitness Careers
Food Services
Foreign Language Careers
Forestry Careers
Gerontology Careers
Government Service
Graphic Communications
Health and Medical Careers
High Tech Careers
Home Economics Careers
Hospital Administration
Hotel & Motel Management
Human Resources Management
   Careers
Information Systems Careers

Insurance Careers
Interior Design
International Business
Journalism Careers
Landscape Architecture
Laser Technology
Law Careers
Law Enforcement and Criminal Justice
Library and Information Science
Machine Trades
Magazine Publishing Careers
Management
Marine & Maritime Careers
Marketing Careers
Materials Science
Mechanical Engineering
Medical Technology Careers
Metalworking Careers
Microelectronics
Military Careers
Modeling Careers
Music Careers
Newspaper Publishing Careers
Nursing Careers
Nutrition Careers
Occupational Therapy Careers
Office Occupations
Opticianry
Optometry
Packaging Science
Paralegal Careers
Paramedical Careers
Part-time & Summer Jobs
Performing Arts Careers
Petroleum Careers
Pharmacy Careers
Photography
Physical Therapy Careers
Physician Careers
Plastics Careers
Plumbing & Pipe Fitting
Podiatric Medicine
Printing Careers
Property Management Careers
Psychiatry
Psychology
Public Health Careers
Public Relations Careers
Purchasing Careers
Real Estate
Recreation and Leisure
Refrigeration and Air Conditioning
Religious Service
Restaurant Careers
Retailing
Robotics Careers
Sales Careers
Sales & Marketing
Secretarial Careers
Securities Industry
Social Science Careers
Social Work Careers
Speech-Language Pathology Careers
Sports & Athletics
Sports Medicine
State and Local Government
Teaching Careers
Technical Communications
Telecommunications
Television and Video Careers

Theatrical Design & Production
Transportation Careers
Travel Careers
Trucking Careers
Veterinary Medicine Careers
Vocational and Technical Careers
Welding Careers
Word Processing
Writing Careers
Your Own Service Business

CAREERS IN Accounting; Advertising;
Business; Communications; Computers;
Education; Engineering; Health Care;
Law; Marketing; Science

CAREER DIRECTORIES
Careers Encyclopedia
Occupational Outlook Handbook

CAREER PLANNING
Admissions Guide to Selective
   Business Schools
Career Planning and Development for
   College Students and Recent
   Graduates
Careers Checklists
Careers for Animal Lovers
Careers for Bookworms
Careers for Foreign Language
   Aficionados
Careers for Good Samaritans
Careers for Sport Nuts
Careers for Travel Buffs
Guide to Basic Resume Writing
Handbook of Business and
   Management Careers
Handbook of Scientific and
   Technical Careers
How to Change Your Career
How to Choose the Right Career
How to Get and Get Ahead
   On Your First Job
How to Get People to Do Things
   Your Way
How to Have a Winning Job Interview
How to Land a Better Job
How to Make the Right Career Moves
How to Prepare for College
How to Run Your Own Home Business
How to Succeed in High School
How to Write a Winning Resume
Joyce Lain Kennedy's Career Book
Life Plan
Planning Your Career of Tomorrow
Planning Your College Education
Planning Your Military Career
Planning Your Young Child's
   Education
Resumes for Communications Careers
Resumes for High Tech Careers
Resumes for Sales and Marketing Careers

SURVIVAL GUIDES
Dropping Out or Hanging In
High School Survival Guide
College Survival Guide

VGM Career Horizons
a division of *NTC Publishing Group*
4255 West Touhy Avenue
Lincolnwood, Illinois 60646-1975